Evil Invades Sanctuary

The Case for Security
in
Faith-Based Organizations

Carl Chinn

www.carlchinn.com

Printed by   Snowl
                        www.snowl

Cover designed by   **Robin Montoya**
                        www.cleanclipart.com

Disclaimer on incident stories;
Extensive effort has been made to verify the accuracy in each story and suggestion. Incident information is gathered from major news syndicates, law enforcement press releases, and public court records. While great care is taken with the wording of each incident, a certain margin of error exists in any collection of stories. I welcome any corrective suggestions discovered by readers who were involved in any of the incidents listed, or professionals in the protection community. Accuracy is critical as we learn from the historical register of criminal actions in religious environments. Neither the author, nor any others associated with this book can be held liable for mistakes.

Printed in the United States of America

First Edition. 2012

ISBN-10: 0615657885

ISBN-13: 978-0-615-65788-2

Many people of faith still find it unthinkable to believe that a person with violent intent will come into their midst at their place of worship or ministry. Coming face to face with this reality twice, Carl Chinn has chosen to devote over fifteen years to researching and documenting others who have been thrust into this same scenario for the purpose of sounding the trumpet to faith-based organizations. Once you have reviewed Carl's evidence, the answer to the question -- "Could it happen here?" -- is an absolute "Yes!"

Dave Johnson, Facilities/Security Director,
Woodmen Valley Chapel, Colorado Springs, CO

CONTENTS

About This Book
&
Those Who Helped

As the driver was transporting me from the airport to the church where I was to speak, he asked about the conference subject. I told him it was about security in faith-based organizations.

He said that was a subject he had often considered, but concluded that security in church is like a busy intersection in need of a traffic light. Many observe the need and talk about it, but little gets done until somebody gets hurt. He was spot on.

Evil Invades Sanctuary is not a how-to book; it is a literary journey confirming the need for security in faith-based organizations. As you travel it, I hope you discover applicable insights to develop an effective and intentional security program for your organization.

It tells the stories of those involved in deadly force incidents in such a way to help others (both law enforcement and civilian alike) understand what goes on inside such a scene.

Evil has invaded sanctuary, and will do so again.

Acknowledgements

Many have helped develop and edit this book and contributed to the professionalism of it.

Many of those are in the ministry security business. Chuck Chadwick, Raleigh Rhodes, Jimmy Meeks, Den Patterson, and Jeff Kowell have contributed directly, indirectly, or simply by the momentum of affiliation and discussions.

Many current or prior law enforcement officers have significantly influenced my views. Don Shannon, Todd Evans, Jake Shirk and Charlie Hess deserve special mention. None in law enforcement have impacted me as much as my own brother, Vernon Chinn.

Many church crime victims or witnesses have become friends; many of whom contributed edits. In order of timing of their deadly force experiences in a church setting are John Bauers, Larry Linam, David Works, John Bohstedt and Tommy Ishmael. My sincere appreciation to those of you who were there and shared your stories with me. A special thanks to Jeff Laster who walked me through the Wedgewood Baptist Church showing me how that awful shooting transpired. All of you from Daingerfield, TX – what an incredible experience you went through in 1980. Thank you all for taking time for me.

David Works, Garvin McCarrell and Brady Boyd reviewed the New Life shooting sections, and countless friends have reviewed other portions as well. Jeff Kohr not only edited the writing, he donated a large bore tactical weapon to me (you will understand when you read chapter 5).

Every one of our children (and their spouses) endured "what do you think of this?" sessions, and offered their edits and comments in response. My older brother, Ed Chinn (Author of <u>Footprints in</u>

the Sea), contributed many edits and helped me understand the business of writing.

Rachel Thomas diligently reviewed and professionally edited the final version. Her finishing professional touches were needed to nudge it across the finish line.

Thank you all and many more who should be named.

Thanks most of all to my wife, Deana. Not only did she edit, re-edit, and edit every version again through the years, she paid the highest price in my significant absences as I would disappear downstairs for hours (and sometimes days) of researching and writing. Often when I was right beside her, she knew I really wasn't. She has often seen me in the book even when it wasn't in my hands.

But I wrote it for all of you. I hope the stories are expressed well enough to pass on this passion.

Foreword

As I read Carl's detailed description of May 2nd, 1996, I couldn't help but return to that time so permanently etched into many of our memories. It was on that day that an angry and bitter man walked into our "sanctuary" with the intent of evil. Focus on the Family was under siege by a solo gunman, as we prepared to seek the provision and protection from our God on the National Day of Prayer! We truly experienced the promise of Proverbs 18:10 (NASB) that day; "**The name of the LORD is a strong tower; The righteous runs into it and is safe**." I will remember in detail His great provision and protections as the whole nation turned to our plight in prayer!

Carl Chinn was one of those provisions and blessings of the Lord. Let me simply say that Carl is a man who men want around in a time of need. His dedication to service and attention to detail are his trademark. But for me, May 2nd revealed Carl as a true man's man, offering his safety and potentially his life for others. It was a deed that emerged from his inner man, without requiring thought. It revealed who he truly is at the core of his being, a humble hero and a servant. Carl displays the promise of Ephesians 3:16 (NASB), "**that He would grant you, according to the riches of His glory, to be strengthened with power through His Spirit in the inner man**".

Things went well for us that day, due to the Love of God, the character of His man, and prior preparation and planning. The costs had been weighed in advance, the plans had been laid out, and the LORD blessed His people.

In *Evil Invades Sanctuary*, Carl Chinn makes a case for Faith Based organizations to consider making their plans and preparations to protect those in their care. In our case the basic elements were as simple as an alarm system and practiced evacuation routines. In the end we all acknowledge it was the

v

LORD who acted on our behalf through the preparations that had been established. In Proverbs 16:3 (NASB) we read, "**Commit your works to the LORD And your plans will be established**".

That is the clear and compelling message of this book. I would encourage many to read what Carl has written, take it to the LORD in prayer, and develop your plan as HE instructs you.

Thanks, Carl. Your servant heart and bravery have made you a true hero to me. I pray that you will never again experience the senseless violence you have witnessed, and that your lessons learned will help many others avoid it as well.

Stanley John
Senior Vice President
Global Ministry
Focus on the Family

CHAPTER 1
The Wakeup Call

"Get your people out of the building or I will bring it down -- I have the explosives, and I will do it now!" As his profanities boomed through the big lobby, I saw the initial expressions of bewilderment from those around him. Then they began running out of the building as he undressed, revealing ominous ink scribbles on his bare upper torso -- instructions to the coroner regarding his body when the day was done.

As I witnessed his rage, I kept a watchful eye on the Walther pistol in his right hand and a pile of stuffed green military packs on the floor in front of him, in which he claimed were enough explosives to destroy the building. I could see what appeared to be small white wires going from the loaded pack material to a trigger device in his unstable left hand. He had taken two female receptionists hostage; I will never forget the way the women trembled. It was obvious this was no joke, and equally clear that my day's priorities had just been changed.

It wasn't the kind of scene one would typically see or hear in the normally peaceful lobby of Focus on the Family, a non-profit ministry intended to provide hope to families through biblical principles.

I worked for Focus through the development and construction of their campus in Colorado Springs. We had just finished the installation of a new panic alert system when this incident happened. When the alert sounded on my radio, I thought a receptionist was checking to see what would happen if she activated it.

Life is full of details which may not fit the larger narrative. Adrenaline burns some things into memory, distorts some, and loses some after a significant emotional event. That morning I had ripped my pants out. Too busy to go home, I called my wife to bring me another pair.

1

Laughing, she discretely picked me up behind one of the buildings. After changing clothes in the mini-van, we went to lunch. We kissed goodbye as she dropped me back off at Focus at 1:10 PM.

Seventeen minutes later, my radio alarm sounded.

I am sure there are many who can recall similar stories of what they were doing before the day changed. In Colorado Springs, many were going about their business with no clue that an angry man awoke that morning, deciding "this is the day."

Perhaps as he lit the first marijuana joint in his apartment, the receptionists – who would later become his hostages – were straightening the reception counter so it would look nice for the day's guests. As he began writing those eerie messages on his skin, Focus employees in accounting, shipping, broadcasting and other departments were assuming their normal routines. As he was walking the last miles from where the taxi dropped him off, parents were walking their children through the Focus on the Family story-book rooms filled with pictures of "Mr. Whitaker" and the other familiar child entertainment characters.

He walked past a gardener who smiled and greeted him as she was weeding a flower bed. He passed by without a word as the soundtrack of "Natural Born Killers" hammered his mind through his Walkman's earphones. None of us had any way of knowing what plans were developing against us.

Just because we didn't know the details didn't mean we were unprepared. Procedures were in place, initial responders trained, and an automatic alert system established. Most importantly, we were not naïve about the possibilities.

Though the investigation revealed he had planned the attack for years, there were some things the gunman did not know that day. He did not know about a memo that had been written exactly one year earlier, on

2

May 2nd, 1995. Prompted by an internal investigation following the April 19th Oklahoma City bombing, that memo requested some simple security upgrades. The panic alert system was one of those upgrades.

And the gunman did not know that this day -- May 2nd, 1996 -- was the National Day of Prayer.

• • •

"Faith-based" should not mean "easy target"

The hostage situation at Focus on the Family was certainly not the first violent crime that happened at a U.S. ministry. It was however one of the more widely publicized incidents to date, due in part to the broadcast nature and international audience of that particular ministry. Because of the media exposure of that incident, it was one of the first well-known incidents confirming the value of effective security planning in a faith-based organization.

Ten and a half years later, and just two and a half miles north of the Focus facility, another angry gunman invaded New Life Church. He too was stopped short of his plans of carnage by actions of a team that was prepared.

I was extensively involved in the pre-incident emergency response planning at both ministries, and was in the hallway as an initial responder in both incidents. Key to the successful responses at both ministries was their willingness to accept responsibility for the safety of their people years earlier. Both ministries had people, parts and plans in place.

Through the years, my work has focused a great deal on church and Para-church ministries. I often encounter a low level of priority given to emergency preparedness by such organizations. Some ministries are of course better prepared than others, but security is often not a priority at ministries until something significant happens. Fortunately that was not the case at Focus on the Family or New Life Church.

Focus on the Family had endured a history of smaller incidents. They experienced the common misbehaviors associated with the human dynamics of employees. They were also a lightning rod for the occasional resentment of opposing viewpoints due to the controversial nature of Dr. James Dobson's very passionate and publicized stands on sensitive issues. There had been threats, vandalism and even occasional invasions from some of the aggrieved parties. All of this contributed to the historical folder of information confirming the need for intentional incident readiness. One of the most significant incidents that contributed to emergency preparation at Focus on the Family was the Oklahoma City bombing. We paid special attention to the tragedy, processed various scenarios, and developed plans accordingly.

Incidents had occurred at New Life Church through the years as well. Among many lesser known incidents, this was the church planted, nurtured and led by Ted Haggard, whose secret life of gay sex and methamphetamine use surprised the nation in 2006. Long before Haggard's shocking misconduct was exposed, there was a functioning emergency response team there as well.

Both ministries were paying attention to what was happening close to them and throughout America, and were better prepared on the day of their attacks. The experiences of these Colorado ministries are a contribution of lessons learned regarding security readiness and response in ministry environments.

Incidents such as these reveal the crucial need for intentional security for all churches whether their membership is 50 or 5,000 people (the Brookefield Wisconsin church where Terry Ratzmann opened fire killing 7, then himself on March 12, 2005 had only 50 people in the service). This is not just a church issue; it is important to any faith-based organizations such as a radio ministry, publisher, school, medical facility, shelter or charitable outreach.

Historically, the majority of violent aggression has been directed at individuals or small groups of people known by the attacker. Over the past four decades however, America has seen an increasing frequency of attacks aimed at larger groups of people unknown to the attacker. One of the first of these random attacks was the August 1, 1966 University of Texas shooting when Charles Whitman shot forty-five people (killing fourteen and wounding thirty-one). Between 1966 and October 16, 1991 when George Hennard gunned down forty-five (twenty-three of whom died) in a Luby's Cafeteria in Killeen, Texas, there were few other such incidents. Since 1991 there has been a significant increase in the frequency of such violence against crowds; occurring in malls, office buildings, schools, open roads, open spaces and churches.

According to the U.S. Department of Justice, homicides involving *groups of victims* increased (as a ratio of total homicides) by 42% from 1976 to 2005 (homicides by *groups of offenders* in the same analysis increased by 76.5% in the same time period)[1]. Many *spree killers* such as Eric Harris (Columbine) and Seung-Hui Cho (Virginia Tech) shared a driving hatred of faith which is contagious to group or individual extremists. It is just a matter of time before we see another mass attack in a religious setting.

In addition to significant acts of domestic aggression is the increasing reality of international terrorists. In the preface of the 9/11 Commission Report, the investigative team delivered a chilling description of a very determined enemy;

> *We learned about an enemy who is sophisticated, patient, disciplined and lethal...its hostility toward us and our values is limitless. Its purpose is to rid the world of religious and political pluralism, the plebiscite and equal rights for women[2].*

Faith-based organizations are in the direct line of fire in the battle raging between good and evil. Whether from terrorists, petty criminals, fallen leaders or hurricanes, religious organizations must prepare for adversity. In addition to large scale risks such as shooters and terrorists, faith-based organizations must increase their awareness of, and preparation for, accidental, criminal, or environmental hazards capable of compromising their primary purpose.

Unlike other organizations, bible-based entities struggle with the perceived conflict between divine protection and active security planning. But there is no conflict; just because we pray for God's protection before driving does not mean we speed or dismiss the value of seatbelts. Likewise, faith-based organizations must intentionally provide for the safety of staff and visitors.

• • •

The Value of Vigilance

Mom was a Sunday school teacher. I recall how she told the story of Gideon's fight with the Midianites. With the odds already stacked against Gideon by sheer numbers, the Lord wanted him to engage the enemy with even *fewer* men so there would be no doubt as to Who truly saved the day. The Lord directed Gideon to select the men by watching how they drank water.

I remember how we were spellbound first-graders as she read Judges 7: 5-7;

> *So Gideon took the men down to the water. There the LORD told him, "Separate those who lap the water with their tongues like a dog from those who kneel down to drink." Three hundred men lapped with their hands to their mouths. All the rest got down on their knees to drink. The LORD said to Gideon, "With the three hundred men that lapped I will save you and give the Midianites into your hands. Let all the other men go, each to his own place."*

I will never forget how Mom dramatically mimicked a dog lapping water. She delivered a lasting impression of how dogs lay their head almost flat over the water and dip their tongues into it, never taking their eyes away from constant searching for action.

According to Mom, the other men were making everyone vulnerable as they dropped to their knees and looked straight down into the water, laughing and talking as if there were no danger around. Her obvious point was that the Lord is looking for people who are vigilant.

Vigilance is always crucial; attentiveness results in awareness.

On the quiet afternoon of September 7th, 1876, a young man by the name of Henry Wheeler was home in Northfield, Minnesota taking leave from his medical studies at Michigan University. Sitting under an awning in front of his father's store across from the bank, he watched three strangers ride into town. He saw them stop at the bank and throw their reins over the hitching posts. *But they did not tie the reins.* Other similar observations resulted in him and others being ready when the first shots were fired by the bad guys in the bank. When the incident was over, the Jesse James / Cole Younger gang would never ride together again. Common townspeople foiled one of the most notorious gangs in U.S. history, because a college student noticed the reins weren't tied.

Pray and Protect

Had young Henry Wheeler simply *noticed* that the reins were untied, and did nothing about it, the results would have been different. More people would have died in future bank robberies from the violent gang.

A new phrase has become common in recent years with law enforcement -- *actionable intelligence.* It's not a new concept -- it's just been recently well named. Henry Wheeler and the other citizens of Northfield, Minnesota were not the first ones to act on intelligence.

7

When Nehemiah was rebuilding the walls of Jerusalem, he heard that enemies were coming. He gave us a great model for ministry security (and acting on the intelligence gathered) when he wrote,

> ...*we prayed to our God AND posted a guard day and night...*[3], and *Those who carried materials did their work with one hand and held a weapon with the other, and each of the builders wore his sword at his side...*[4]

I am not suggesting that our religious establishments should resemble NORAD. I am not urging ushers to wear Colt .45s, or suggesting bomb scanners be installed in nurseries. I am suggesting we have a responsibility to be prepared. We must initiate appropriate security measures and not be complacent in the face of very real threats.

To make a site or facility unappealing for criminal access is to *harden* the target. In contrast, a place attractive to criminals is a *soft* (easy) target. As a nation we are in the process of hardening targets (schools, airports, public buildings, etc.). That process is accelerated after significant attacks such as Oklahoma City, Columbine or 9/11. As targets are hardened, safe places for criminal acts diminish. The result of more hardened targets is an inevitable increase of crime around soft targets.

Religious organizations have lagged behind by discounting security, luring more criminal activity toward churches and other religious groups. It is time to harden faith-based targets in measured steps.

• • •

Start with what you have

Ministries and faith-based organizations of all sizes already have most of what they need for safety and security. I recommend starting with what you have, and as other people, parts or processes are needed, merge them into the developing program. Preparation can be many things -- from simply being aware, to fancy gadgets and binder-sized plans and everything between. Regardless of the size and complexity of the plan, ministries should be prepared at all times.

While staying simple, security decisions should be intentional. For example I park my vehicle at a certain place, aimed in a specific direction. I set my dome light so it will not come on (in a crisis situation I do not want the light revealing my position). I sit in a particular place for a specific reason during Sunday service. Clothing, schedule, physical and mental posturing should always be intentional.

According to the Hartford Institute for Religion Research, there are 336,000 congregations in the United States. Only 1,300 of those are considered to be a "mega-church" (over 2,000 members). 59% have between 7 and 99 congregants, and only 6% have over 500 people in their membership. It is not the size that matters. While large churches may be more of a lightning rod for controversy, or those with a propensity for national recognition of violence, it only takes 33 to set a new record of shooting victims. On a chilling note, pedophiles may be more likely to attend a small rural church than a large metropolitan one. All they need is one child.

Any size church or faith-based organization should put in place some level of intentional security. At the very least, they should appoint someone to *own* organizational safety. In a large organization this may be a hired position, while in a smaller congregation it may be a family member of the pastor or an usher. But someone should be recognized as the one who owns the process. Every organization can improve their program as they learn and grow, but the important thing is to recognize the need, then do something about it.

This book is a threat awareness message specifically for ministries. It is about physical protection and practical vigilance in a society where evil has invaded sanctuary, and will do so again.

In the aftermath of the shooting at our church, New Life Church hired a seasoned police psychologist to council the four of us who were the primary initial security responders. In my counseling sessions with Doctor T. he said New Life had just established the *Coping Model* for church security. Not knowing what a coping model was, I had to ask.

A coping model is the demonstration of experience overcoming a particular difficulty.

I wish we hadn't experienced what we did at New Life in 2007 or at Focus in 1996. But because we did, I hope our experiences may serve as a coping model as others navigate through the issues associated with the reality that bad things happen in good places.

CHAPTER 2
Think About it

Before 9/11/01 airline crews were instructed simply to cooperate with the demands of hijackers. The model of hijackers capitalizing on that quiet compliance to use the plane as a suicide bomb had never happened. It is not a bad mark against the crews and passengers of the first three planes that day that they didn't take action. They complied as most would have, given the models to go by. It is really quite remarkable that the passengers and crew of flight 93 so quickly created the new model.

Now airline protocol (as well as passenger response) is different, and because of that difference Richard Reid now shares prison with the likes of Ted Kaczynski instead of sharing history with Mohamed Atta. Flight attendants and passengers took 6' 4" Reid down hard with creative weapons of seatbelt extensions, headphones and brute force as he tried to bring down American Airlines flight 63 over the Atlantic shortly after 9/11 with a deadly bomb hidden in his shoe.

Just as law enforcement agencies, schools and airlines learn and adapt from incidents, churches should do the same. Threats are endless and unpredictable, as are their *triggers* (reasons for the attacks). The triggers offered for heinous examples following are not spiritual theories. That angle can be written by someone else. These are simply the reasons discovered in the investigations.

On April 27th, 2003 Daniel Bondeson laced arsenic into the coffee in the Gustaf Adolph Lutheran Church in New Sweden, Maine. Walter Reid Morrill died, and 15 others were hospitalized as a result of the poisoning. It was discovered to have been retaliation over petty church politics, personal grudges, and being offended by nasty tasting coffee at a previous church event.

On April 25th, 2008 an argument over damaged mailboxes erupted in the parking lot of the Pinedale Baptist Church in Ashville, Alabama leaving one man shot and killed.

In Wheaton, Minnesota on September 3, 2009 Claude Hankins and David Collins got into a fight in the sanctuary of Thy Kingdom Come World Ministry over a washer and dryer. Collins swung a baseball bat at Hankins hitting Hankins's 14 month old daughter instead, killing her.

At a party on March 11th, 2011 at the Bethlehem United Methodist Church Community Center in Edin, North Carolina, Eric Blackstock and Akeen Laquan Clark got into an argument over the best place to live in the area. Clark produced a handgun and shot Blackstock in the chest.

Some motives are more comprehensible than others in this review of ministry environment incidents. Some are well known, some more obscure, but all can be considered an unpredictable array of possibilities of emergency situations affecting ministries. To be aware of the unpredictable nature of a criminal is to be better prepared to protect people and property.

In addition to differences of perception and interpretation concerning *why*, is the fact that not all criminals tell the truth (imagine that). So what we have to work with as we consider explanations of *why*, is a journey through opinions, excuses, legal discoveries (often spun by attorneys driven more by case success than a quest for truth), and other forms of smoke. The reasons are informative, sometimes based on conjecture, and almost amusing at times as we consider the limitless range of *why* someone carried out an evil act. What may not appear as reasonable cause for a given action to you may be entirely defensible to someone with a criminal disposition (or true insanity). As Robert Browne (incarcerated serial killer) told my good friend Charlie Hess (co-author of the book, "Hello Charlie – Letters From a Serial Killer"), "what's important to you is not important to me."[5]

How can you determine when someone walks through the door of your facility where their mind is at? How do you know who or what may have set them off? It may not have anything to do with your place as the source of the retaliation. Often an offense simply came from an obscure church member or stranger. Ministry leadership was often not aware of, nor did they have any control or influence over the situation until it exploded under their roof or in their parking lot.

In many deadly force incidents at churches and ministries however, there was at least some level of observation of the brewing storm. But for various reasons it wasn't taken seriously until it was too late and became an investigation.

I have tracked all deadly force incidents I could discover which occurred in or on the properties of faith-based organizations in the US since 1999. In developing the resulting statistics, I was particularly interested in trends that could be used in effective situational awareness and crime prevention.

Review www.carlchinn.com for current statistics and stories of deadly force incidents at faith-based organizations

The triggers are a primary item of interest in that regard. While my website is a better source to keep an eye on that dynamic data, the following gives a good preview of trigger statistics relating to 497 deadly force incidents occurring at those ministries in the 13 years from 1999 through 2011.

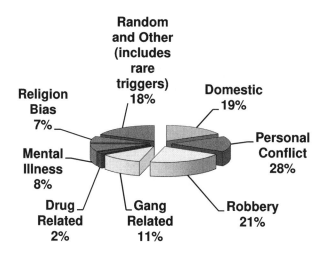

Religion Bias 7%

Mental Illness 8%

Random and Other (includes rare triggers) 18%

Domestic 19%

Personal Conflict 28%

Drug Related 2%

Gang Related 11%

Robbery 21%

While a deadly force incident remains one of the least likely incidents to occur at any given church, this research has verified that it is a much more common thing than previously thought. Among other statistics discovered are the following (for 1999-2011):

- Some deadly force attacks had the potential for death, but death did not occur. However 215 (43.26%) of these attacks were an attack resulting in the death of others (ARDO).

- 10 (4.65%) ARDO's were stopped by law enforcement and 9 (4.19%) were stopped by others. **91.16% of the time the killer didn't stop until they decided to stop.**

- Of 279 total victim deaths (including suspicious deaths), 173 (62.01%) were male, and 106 (37.99%) were female.

- 59.67% of these attacks occurred during non-event times (including office hours of a church when no event was going on).

- 27.27% of the attacks were by more than one attacker.

- **66.12% of these attacks occurred outside the building on church grounds or an off-site event.**

- The following statistics relate to the aggressors themselves (suicide is considered an aggressor whether they killed others or not):

  - 92.09% were male

  - 24.54 % were known to have been affiliated (member, past member, employee, volunteer, vendor) with the ministry

  - 9.6% committed suicide (many of which killed others first)

  - 2.79% were killed by those intervening

  - 55.67% were arrested

  - 31.94% are unknown or at large

- Of 513 known attack weapons (some weapons were never known, some attacks had multiple weapons) the following indicates the frequency of weapon choices:

  - 59.26% were firearms

  - 17.15% were knives or other stabbing weapons

  - 5.26% were explosives (counting Molotov cocktails)

  - 2.53% were vehicular assault or homicide

- 15.79% were various other weapons and means (poison, beating, hanging, fire, various objects)

Statistics can be like theology – you can usually find or manipulate one (or a collection) to support what you want to prove or already believe. Regardless of how you crunch these statistics, sufficient data exists to support the need for intentional safety and security awareness in ministries.

Some have made the point that one is more likely to be killed by lightning than by violence at church. We're far more likely to die in a car accident than in criminal violence as well, but that doesn't mean we stop violence awareness and readiness. Lightning safety is common and observed in regions prone to the dangers – as it should be. Consider the following points:

- There was an average of 82 deaths per year attributed to lightning in the United States between 1980 and 1995[6].

- In 2009, there were 34 violent deaths at church, while no children died in a school fire.

- Between 1980 and 2005, there was only an average of 1.5 deaths per year in American school fires[7].

- There was an annual average of 28 deaths caused by violence in American K-12 schools from school year 1992-1993 until school year 2007-2008[8].

- There was an annual average of 24 deaths caused by violence in churches and ministries in the 13 year time period of church violence from 1999-2011.

It would be wrong to suggest we stop training and drilling school children on safety in the event of fire or violent attacks. Fire safety awareness for schools has been quite effective at preventing school fire deaths in the last 50 years. Violent deaths at schools averaged over 38 per year from the '92 – '93 school years up through the '98 – '99 year.

Since Columbine, and the focus on school safety programs and violence prevention training, the average number of annual violent deaths has fallen to just over 20 in the years since (even with the 3 consecutive school year spikes from 2002-2005)[9].

We should learn lessons from public school models and apply them to our houses of worship and faith-based organizations as well. The same criminal actions and hazards they face are common to us.

I am often asked, "What is my church's most likely threat?" That depends on regional, historical, cultural and other specific experiences of any particular ministry. In addition to these variables is the message of the subject ministry. Regardless of which incident may be most likely at any given place, the benefits of improved awareness and preparedness apply to all such incidents.

Medical emergencies, lost children, domestic disputes, juvenile imprudence, personal conflicts, theft, general social instability and misplaced vehicles in the parking lot would all be consistently expected incident categories in a normal church. Physical or mental abuse by a person in charge or child to child is a far more common problem than many are prepared for.

Exploring the unpredictable range of hazard sources and motivators confirms the need to be prepared for any type of emergency. As strange as it may sound, to train a safety / security team in tornado awareness will help to prepare them for an active shooter. To exercise continuously improving methods of finding lost children will better prepare teams for a fire. Prior to the shooting at New Life, our team's greatest strength was in reconnecting lost children with parents. In a church with 14,000 in typical weekly attendance -- many of which were first time visitors, the potential for such was significant. We were proud of the fact that our average re-unite time was about one minute. So the following incidents offer things to think about. As they are considered, keep in mind that it only takes three elements for any violent crime:

1) An attacker motivated by a cause

2) A victim who represents that cause

3) A lack of protection

The first two elements exist in just about any major gathering of people. The third may be more common in faith-based organizations than any other group.

• • •

FIRE

The horror of hatred is often seen in fire. It is part of the psyche of the most violent criminal minds. Hate is the source of most crimes of violence against people or groups, showing its ugliness quite frequently through flame and explosion.

Arson and bombings are frequent tools of hate used against ministry environments. Nationwide there were 485,000 structure fires in 2010[10], with 27,000 (5.57%) of them labeled as "intentionally set." This was a fairly typical year.

By the same research (NFPA), there was an average of 1,890 U.S. Religious and Funeral Property Structure Fires per year during 2004 -- 2008. But in those structure types, the intentionally set ratio is nearly three times the average (15%) accounting for 26% of the loss value[11].

Arson and related attacks on ministries have been an increasing concern at the federal level. In 1996 Congress formed the NCATF (National Church Arson Task Force). The NCATF coordinates federal, state and local law enforcement activities when church related arsons or bombing attacks occur. It is now chaired by the ATF (Bureau of Alcohol Tobacco and Firearms). The ATF leads the investigations and criminal apprehensions. Other agencies which make up this task force are the Federal Bureau of Investigation, Department of Justice, Federal Emergency Management Administration, and Housing and Urban Development.

The NCATF dispatches their National Response Team to investigate ministry fires, bombings, and certain other indiscretions, usually within 24 hours of the attack. This team, backed by all the training and technology of the participating agencies, is comprised of chemistry, canine and explosives specialists. The NCATF defines their battlefield in this war on hatred by stating, "Those who would attack our churches seek to strike at our most fundamental liberties and sources of support."[12] They clearly have the same vision as I for writing this book, and as you for reading it.

Be aware that any fire or talk of fire or explosives around your ministry should result in immediate security attention. The following story is one of the most tragic examples of an attack on an American church. The stench of this smoke still repulses any decent human decades after it happened.

When there is controversy, there are radicals inclined to carry it to the extreme. In 1963 the prevalent controversy was racial equality.

By the fall of 1963, the 16th Street Baptist Church in Birmingham, Alabama had become a center of activity for the racial equality movement. Well known civil rights activists Martin Luther King Jr., Ralph Abernathy and Fred Shuttlesworth were regular guests. Two of the organizations frequently meeting there -- the Southern Christian Leadership Conference (SCLC) and the Congress on Racial Equality

(CORE) -- were gaining momentum in the struggle to allow African-Americans to vote in upcoming Birmingham elections.

Opposition was gaining momentum as well. Desegregation of schools was a topic of discord coming to a boil, having been signed into law on September 4th of that year. Alabama Governor George Wallace told a New York Times reporter on September 5th, that our country needed a "few first class funerals" to stop the desegregation he was personally so opposed to. Enforcement of desegregation required National Guard intervention in Birmingham, Mobile, and Tuskegee on September 12th.

In clandestine circles, hatred was fueling anger. As groups of extremists urged each other on, someone probably said, "We should stop talking and do something." The public will never know specifics of how hatred driven discussion turned into deadly action, but it did. Four members of the Birmingham area KKK – Robert Chambliss, Herman Cash, Thomas Blanton and Bobby Cherry decided it was time to stop the progress of racial equality.

On Sunday morning, September 15th regular church services were under way at the 16th Street Baptist Church. As a long-standing tradition, it was "Youth Sunday" where children were to lead the 11:00 AM adult service. As they prayed around 10:20 AM in preparation for the service (which would have been entitled, "The Love That Forgives") approximately 19 sticks of dynamite erupted in a massive blast. 11-year-old Denise McNair and 14-year-olds Cynthia Wesley, Carole Robertson and Addie Mae Collins were killed -- one of them decapitated by the blast.

Witnesses testified later they had seen a Chevrolet pull up, a man place a box under the east stairs, then get back in the car that raced away just moments before the blast.

The 16th Street Baptist Church remains strong today. As I write this we have come so far as a nation from this level of wicked contempt, it is inconceivable to most Americans. We have progressed so far beyond the black vote issue that we voted in a black man as President of the United States. Though we would have rather seen those little girls grow up and have their own families, we as a nation owe a debt of gratitude to them and to the 16th Street Baptist Church.

THINK ABOUT IT:

- The church was "on the move" with a very direct message of needed change.

- There was no active exterior security presence.

- Bobby Cherry had attacked Fred Shuttlesworth at least once before -- at a Birmingham school in 1957.

- The church had been receiving bomb threats and there were three bombings in Birmingham in the four weeks prior to this blast. All of this had caused the church to emphasize its message, but not to plan against specific threats.

- In spite of the seriousness of the times, there was no effort made (that we are aware of) to hire extra-duty law enforcement officers. On a sad note, due to the racism of the times it may have been difficult (if not impossible) to obtain such protection.

- The attackers had investigated the site prior to the attack, but on the day of the attack were on site for mere seconds – all that was needed to place the bomb.

MOLESTATION, ABUSE, PORNOGRAPHY, SEXUAL MISCONDUCT

This is the most difficult category for me to grasp. If denial were a good thing (it isn't) I may be inclined to choose (as many ministry leaders have done for years) to deny that this could ever happen in my church or in yours. History tells us however that this is certainly no arena to bury our heads in the sand about. Consider for instance that 37% of pastors surveyed confessed to involvement in "inappropriate sexual behavior with someone in the church." [13]

How can we determine and intervene when someone is venturing past that line in the scale of progression from natural thoughts becoming perversion, and finally morphing into inappropriate sexual behavior?

We can't, but what we can do is to make certain there are protective and preventive measures in place in our respective ministries. Forget all mindsets about what abuse is -- it can happen from a 20-year-old to an 80-year-old, reverse of that, and any range in between or beyond. Male to female, female to male, male to male, female to female, group to child, child to child. Sure, statistics evidence more adult male to child female crimes in this category, but the bottom line is that abuse -- especially of the sexual nature -- can be very damaging to the victim. It is far more common than we want to acknowledge.

We've all heard of those who, when caught in such impropriety blame their own behavior on some personal incident from their youth. That may be true in some cases. With the infamous fall of Ted Haggard, that was part of his story. He had allegedly been molested by one of his dad's employees when he was a small boy, which had an impact.

But this is my book, and in it I won't let anyone off the hook of personal responsibility by tagging their victimization as justification for their disgusting behavior. Many of us personally know others who experienced such trauma as a young person who wouldn't begin to entertain thoughts of reciprocating it on anyone else.

Few have been forced through the gauntlet of developing effective child protection in faith-based settings like the Catholic Church. Those who think or suggest that the problem of abuse is restricted to the Catholic Church or religious organizations in general, are mistaken, misguided or purposely deceptive. It is an institutional and cultural

22

issue, and tragically far too prevalent in churches, schools, associations, athletics and private homes than it should have ever become. The problem exists in every denomination. To proclaim no need for caution in a particular organization is either ignorance or deliberate cover-up.

The Catholic Church has paved the way for all of us to learn from their efforts to address this atrocity in ministries. Their new policies on the issue of protecting children and young people are profound and provide lessons learned for all walks of faith. Consider their statement regarding those new policies;

> *The Church in the United States is experiencing a crisis without precedent in our times. The sexual abuse of children and young people by some priests and bishops, and the ways in which we bishops addressed these crimes and sins, have caused enormous pain, anger, and confusion. Innocent victims and their families have suffered terribly. In the past, secrecy has created an atmosphere that has inhibited the healing process and, in some cases, enabled sexually abusive behavior to be repeated. As bishops, we acknowledge our mistakes and our role in that suffering, and we apologize and take responsibility for too often failing victims and our people in the past. We also take responsibility for dealing with this problem strongly, consistently, and effectively in the future. From the depths of our hearts, we bishops express great sorrow and profound regret for what the Catholic people are enduring.*
>
> *We, who have been given the responsibility of shepherding God's people, will, with God's help and in full collaboration with our people, continue to work to restore the bonds of trust that unite us. Words alone cannot accomplish this goal. It will begin with the actions we take here in our General Assembly and at home in our dioceses/eparchies.* [14]

In this category I want to emphasize the frequency of such atrocities as opposed to focusing on any one in particular. As I wrote this section, I decided to consider just one day in the news and provide the headlines for stories on just that day. So welcome to a glimpse of my daily research.

News articles on 4/28/09:

- Tracy, California; Investigators now believe the sexual assault resulting in murder of eight-year-old Sandra Cantu by Sunday School teacher Melissa Huckaby took place inside the Clover Road Baptist Church.

- Benton, Arkansas; At least three men have now come forward with reports of having been sexually abused as teenagers by David Kent Price – former music minister of Benton First Baptist Church who was arrested last week.

- Vinton, Virginia; Cases against two former leaders of Heritage Baptist Church are progressing. Former Assistant Pastor Dan Silverman entered a "no contest" plea in charges of sexual abuse of a 12-year old. Former Deacon Dead Stone facing 24 counts involving sexual molestation regarding two children over 13 and one under that age.

- Grand Prairie, Texas; Former Priest of the Immaculate Conception Catholic Church pleads guilty to one count of possession of child pornography. 40-year-old Matthew Bagert was caught by an associate Priest as he was viewing images of a young nude boy on a rectory computer.

THINK ABOUT IT:

- Churches of all faiths need to step up leadership selection, management and accountability procedures in light of this serious issue. In most stories in this category, the issue of negligence on the part of the church was easy to establish by the prosecution.

- This subject has been viewed as a "Catholic problem" by many. It isn't hard to find news stories of all faiths -- Mormon, Islamic, Catholic, Amish, Jewish, and Protestant -- no faith is free of such vile sexual abuse.

- The U.S. Conference of Catholic Bishops now leads the charge in battling this issue. They have published the *Charter for the Protection of Children and Young People*. They maintain the document under *Child and Youth Protection* at http://usccb.org/issues-and-action. It is an excellent template for any faith taking this issue seriously. Every Protestant should read it. It is a profound model developed through painful experience, and can be easily edited to fit any faith. I hope all faiths will become proactive and avoid adding to this tragic list of victims.

- Become familiar with Boy Scouts of America, Codes of Conduct. There are many applicable models for a church in there as well (see especially article IV, items 10: "the 2 deep rule" & 11: "the rule of 3"). This is also maintained on a publicly accessible website at http://www.orgsites.com/ia/ankenytroop85.

Upon learning of me writing of such things, my good friend Vic Meyer of Tulsa, Oklahoma added some comments. I know of no other security professional that has walked through this fire in the category of sexual abuse on children in church like Vic has. His story (from a protestant evangelical church) is gripping. Any time he is close to your town it is a journey well worth the effort to go hear his presentation on this issue.

Many who have experienced trouble in this field could have avoided it had they followed his three simple thoughts at the first hint of trouble:

1. The process of gaining trust is called "grooming" and involves everyone who could stop the predator. The predator counts on those groomed to find the crime so repugnant that they refuse to believe either the victim or the evidence. For that reason the predator is very likely to be among the most faithful and trusted.

2. There is nothing romantic or consensual about adult on child sexual relationships. It is a crime. Always involve the authorities and eliminate the "groomed effect" from in-house inquiries by selecting people with no relationships to the accused. There is a reason "consensual" is irrelevant under the age of 16.

3. Successful child predators operating in spiritual settings could not do so without the absolute trust of those surrounding them. Trusting friends and co-workers are necessary cogs in the gears that make the predator successful. Those friends and co-workers will be required to give them a pass on policy infractions, dismiss troublesome details, think the best when suspicion is in order and defend when the victim accuses.

CRIMINAL VIOLENCE

It is uncanny how so often following an attack people say, "I knew he would do something like that someday." When Robbie Hawkins went on his shooting rampage in the Omaha Mall in December of 2007, his friends around town began to call each other as they heard the breaking news saying, "I bet this is Robbie." His mother was in an investigator's office as the shooting erupted. When asked if she thought this could be Robbie she didn't want to think so, but the reason she was there visiting with an investigator in the first place was that Robbie had taken an assault rifle from their home and she feared he was going to commit suicide. She was right in that regard -- he did. But not before killing many innocent people in the process.

A security force should, as much as possible, be informed of anyone developing a reputation of suspicion. There is nothing wrong or illegal about recording truthful information about aberrant individuals (or groups) in a "watch list." Law enforcement agencies frequently call it a "BOLO" (be on the lookout). The security team should be well aware of individuals on such a list. Paul told Timothy to look out for Alexander the metalworker, indicating he had done him great harm and would be likely to do the same for Timothy[15]. So this notion of informing security of a potential concern is nothing new.

The investigation of many criminal attacks against ministries where an arrest was made reveals a known history of malcontent of the attacker.

In the hostage situation at Focus on the Family the gunman was angry at some surface issues, while other triggers remain ambiguous theories short of confirmation. Like many criminal acts, it was more the collage of justifications that prompted the attack. Parts of that collage lack confirmation, but the history of malcontent is indisputable.

On October 28th, 1992, we were in the steel erection phase of construction at the 250,000 square foot Focus on the Family headquarters facility. I was on site when an ambulance arrived and took a worker away. The accident scene was fairly gruesome. It was easy to understand how it happened as workers gathering around the site told me about it.

At the bottom of each vertical I-Beam of our building structure, were

5/8" diameter steel reinforcement bars (trade talk calls them "number 5 rebar") protruding up out of the concrete for future tie-in with the concrete floor slab. They all had "OSHA caps" -- big hard orange plastic

27

caps covering the top ends to prevent impaling type injuries should one fall (intended to be protection from a standing height elevation).

I had no idea when I took that picture it would become such a significant topic to me years later, but this was the scene of the accident. Note the rebar protruding up at the base. The flagged one at the end of the pointer is the one talked about next.

Steel workers commonly practice an unsafe activity called "sliding the rail" (OSHA simply categorizes it as "horse-play"). What it means is that when time to come down from high altitude steel erection activities, these workers will sometimes slip down a vertical steel I-beam braking their decent with their legs and gloves in a position similar as one would use in descending a pole. OSHA fines for it, safety officers forbid it, and employers will fire workers caught doing it. But that only challenges the adventurous side of some men.

The injured man was working for a subcontractor under the General Contractor. For whatever reasons, he decided to slide the rail. Unable to control his decent speed, he slipped the 30 feet down the column at almost free fall speed. The OSHA cap was pushed down over the rebar by about 10" as I recall, with chunks of hide and bone cemented to the rebar in blood when I saw it. It impaled him through his posterior.

Worker's Compensation regulations limit benefits to an injured worker when it is determined that an injury was due to horseplay. Such was the case here. As harsh as it may seem, the worker's compensation benefits paid his medical bills but allowed very little compensation for the limited income ability for the rest of his life.

His bitterness and anger over this was directed at every entity he could blame. He became angry at the Workers Compensation Board, his doctors, his attorneys, the General Contractor and the subcontractor he worked for. Eventually his anger turned to the customer the building was being built for -- Focus on the Family. So he decided to return with a gun and a plan. He felt as though all previous efforts for sympathy had failed, and he was going to go out with media coverage of his death designed to expose Focus, the Worker's Compensation system, and everyone else who had *wronged* him.

His wife had left him (taking their children with her) and there was speculation she may have followed principles of Dr. Dobson's "Tough Love" book. But we do know narcotics, depression, and a collection of sympathetic enablers (driven more by political agenda opposed to, or personal hatred against, Focus on the Family than concern for their friend) were sufficient ingredients for an attack recipe.

For several months prior to his attack, he had an illusion (possibly drug induced) that God was instructing him to go to Focus on the Family to make a statement. He became convinced that Focus was to blame for most of his problems, and decided they must pay. He told a Denver newspaper, "I don't know how anyone could be so cruel and consider themselves to be these pristine Christians." In this same interview he indicated that, "this presence came to me -- a light. It wouldn't go away. It told me to go down there." [16]

So on Thursday morning, May 2nd 1996 he went to a Denver church and lit six candles -- one for his wife, one for each of their four children, and one for himself. Then he spent his last $67.00 on a taxi ride to take him *down there.*

His cab fare played out nine miles away, so he walked the rest of the way to Focus on the Family. He walked into the crowded front lobby (being the National Day of Prayer, we had many guests that day). He sat down on a couch area behind the front lobby as the receptionists were greeting multiple visitors. Then, about 1:25 PM he stood up and walked into the lobby booth enclosure.

The lobby booth is surrounded by counter-height walls. The counter portion is on the entry side of the lobby, and the walls continue to enclose a box-like design at the same height as the walk up counter. The back wall of this area is about 12 feet behind the front counter with a waist-high gate -- more to define the area as "staff only" than a secure door.

Once inside the lobby counter area, he tossed bulging military style vest packs on the floor and pulled out a trigger device and wire connected between it and the bags. Then he pulled out the gun, and began shouting at everyone to get out. He would not let the two receptionists go. They discretely enabled the panic system.

I measured my response time to get to the front lobby. I truly thought it was one of the receptionists testing the system. It took only 17 seconds for me to reach the top of the stairs where I could see the lobby desk below. He wasn't yelling when I first saw him, but started again as the responding security guard and I approached him from opposing sides.

Then I saw the gun.

The first thing I felt was utter stupidity. That feeling was one reason I began writing this book on the subject of ministry security. I hope nobody reading this will ever feel as stupid as I did when faced with the real deal. It is sobering to witness concerns you've had unfold in front of you. I hope to help others be prepared for that moment.

He was visibly agitated by the guard to his right and me to his left, both about an arm's length from him. He would swing his chair back and forth as his menacing varied from indiscernible mumbles to angry yells. With his threat of "bringing the building down" he asserted we should get our people out. He became even more enraged as the coil of wire kept falling to the floor as he repeatedly lost control of it.

As other responders entered the scene prompted by the radio alert, one suggested to him we could evacuate everyone by activating the fire alarms, and asked if that was acceptable. He grumbled some sort of approval, so that responder activated the fire alarms. 500 people -- most of whom had no idea what was going on down in the lobby on the lowest level of the big building -- began normal evacuations out the many exits. Many told me later how they thought it was another of my annoying evacuation drills. It was then that those in the immediate area saw as he undressed, showing sinister death messages scrawled on his skin, one of which read, "make sure I'm dead before de-boweling me for a fourth time."

As I stood beside the gunman, I motioned for people to move on and not stop to look or listen. Since I had developed and posted exit routes for the building, I was struck by how few exited past us in the lobby. I later learned some quick thinking initial responders (facility maintenance men) had quickly gone to the areas that would have normally exited out the front lobby and re-directed employees out exits not visible from where our volatile situation was unfolding.

Then -- even with the fire alarms still blaring -- it seemed almost quiet as it became just the four of us; the gunman, his two female hostages, and me. I pointed out to him that everyone was now out of the building and suggested he could now let the two ladies go as well. He adamantly denied my request, despite many ways of attempting to persuade him to do so. He made it very clear that they were not to leave and that I must leave.

I will never forget how violently the ladies trembled as they heard his denial of their freedom. It was as if a violent shaking machine was connected to their chairs. I knew there was no way I could walk out of that scene leaving them alone with him, so I simply asked him to allow me to stay with them (as any man I served with would have done had they been there at that time and observed what I was seeing). My request was granted. It seemed I could do nothing but stand with my arms folded in front of them exhibiting a posture of reassurance. When one of the ladies would look my way, all I could do was smile and give a calming look. They began to calm down.

Not long into the hostage phase, the gunman began to demand that the fire alarms be turned off. Determined to do only what law enforcement wanted (I did not want the gunman making the decisions), I told him I didn't know how (even though I had trained all of our folks on the fire alarm system). I also wanted him to know that his decision to activate the fire alarms would result in first responder agencies arriving, and that I must get instruction from them. This was my way of justifying radio use, and involving law enforcement. He agreed, so I called for the security guard (thinking he could pass his radio to law enforcement, and I could begin dialogue with them).

Instead of answering me on radio, the security guard came walking back into the lobby. It was to be a day of having a plan, then quickly coming up with an alternate plan when that plan didn't go as intended.

The gunman instructed the guard to turn off the fire alarms. I was emphatic to the guard (out of earshot of the gunman) that we not turn them off just because the gunman wanted them off. If law enforcement wanted them on for strategy, I wanted them to stay on. So we called out on radio, and were approved by some authority to go ahead and turn them off, so the guard silenced the alarms.

The guard then positioned himself in the doorway of his office. The gunman instructed the guard to remain where he could see him. Minutes turned to hours as we settled into our positions. The guard was standing to my left with his back against his door jamb facing the gunman. I was standing in front of the lobby counter facing the attacker, with the two ladies seated between him and me. He was seated about four feet away from the ladies who sat facing each other.

The inset following was part of the police report. The arrows indicate the directions faced by the parties throughout the majority of the hostage stage (rectangular insets just indicate flooring type changes).

MB: unnamed security guard
JB & LK: unnamed female hostages
KD: gunman
CC: Carl Chinn

PD: unnamed police sniper

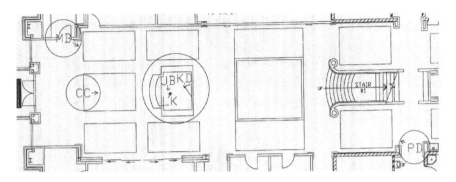

As he would rant meaningless chatter, I would take slow and cautious opportunities to look around. At one point when I looked back over my right shoulder, a SWAT officer in full tactical gear stepped out from behind a column outside by the glass entry, showed me his weapon, nodded reassurance and slipped back into his cover position. It was a significant comfort just knowing the cavalry was there even if we couldn't see them all the time.

That moment was a life-changing experience for me. My views of law enforcement had not been good up until that day. I was no criminal; I just had a bad attitude. I had often remarked that I was paying them (based on my taxes) just so they could pull me over and charge me any time I was going too fast (among similar grumblings).

That gesture by that officer (whom I never met, and still don't know who he was) changed all that. These men and women are ready to do what it takes to protect innocent people, even when they know nothing about those they are willing to step in for.

At some point I noticed the front sight of an M-16 style assault rifle down the hallway to my right (see label of "PD" in the inset). I knew then there were at least two tactical officers close, and that added confidence. I also realized that should this hallway sniper miss, he could easily hit the security guard. As the attacker would look the

33

other way, I would try to whisper to the guard (15 feet or so to my left) that he was "in the line of fire." I tried to get the message to him many times, but was unable to ever do so. After the event was over, the guard disclosed he thought I had been saying, "You should start a fire." He said that made no sense to him – we already had enough trouble and he had no clue why I wanted him to start a fire. It became one of the rare subjects of laughter concerning the incident. I should have known the SWAT sniper was fully aware of his target and surroundings.

The intruder continued to rant about the state worker's compensation board, trying to get the ladies to place a call to them. He was angry that they couldn't dial out on their phones (it was a long distance number he wanted them to dial and the phones at that desk did not have long distance authorization through our switch). He kept saying as soon as he got work comp on the phone, "it would all be over." Not knowing what "it will all be over" meant, I certainly wasn't inclined to disclose to him why the phones wouldn't work.

His ranting would be occasionally interrupted by brief outbursts of mysterious laughter – almost as if he were mentally somewhere else for those moments. But he would quickly return to his angry commentary of all who had wronged him (it was quite a list). As he would seethe his bitterness I would slowly move closer to him with the mic keyed on my radio so some on the outside world could try to make sense of what we were dealing with -- or hear information that may help them in negotiations. But sooner or later he would notice I was too close and order me back. After some time of this back and forth strategy, my radio battery died anyway.

Just before my radio died, I heard someone asking on radio if anyone had the gunman's identity. So I used his desire to make that call as an opportunity to acquire his identity. I fabricated a story of how the fire alarms had disabled the phones, and that I may be able to dial around that feature if he would allow me to come to the phones and try. He agreed.

34

I asked him for the number he wanted me to call. I wrote the number on the back of a business card on the counter, then asked, "Who shall I tell them is calling?" He freely gave me his first, middle and last name, "Kerry Steven Dore."

I knew how to dial our voice mail system in such a way as to prompt an almost angry sounding recording that would scold the user for attempting to use the phones in an unauthorized manner. So while looking at the number and acting as though I was dialing it, I instead dialed up that obnoxious voice in the voice mail system. It was loud enough he could hear it, and I simply hung it back up indicating my attempt to dial around the problem had failed.

I then told him that perhaps the guard could call out on his phone, and asked if I could give the information to him so he could try to contact the folks at the number he had given me. He allowed me to give the information to the guard, who was then able to give his name (and the number he wanted to call) to the rapidly developing command center.

The guard had cleverly positioned himself in such a strategic way that Dore could not see the left side of his body in the doorway to his office. This allowed the guard to use his phone with his left hand, hold it to his ear and talk without Dore seeing it as long as he chose moments Dore was looking away to move his lips. At one point Dr. Dobson himself even called from Washington DC to get an update. The guard told him it just wasn't a good time to discuss the situation.

The phones on the receptionists' counter began to ring (I had to quickly change my fire alarm disabling story to be that the "inbound feature" doesn't disable upon alarm). The receptionists would dutifully and politely answer them, indicate they could not talk right then, and quickly hang up. Dore became increasingly irritated with those annoying calls and jerked the cable out of the wall from one of the phones that had just rang, threw it down on the floor, and began to wreck things on the desk.

In order to stop him from disabling every phone, and to calm him down I told him if he did that to every phone nobody could ever talk, and indicated I had an idea to keep them from ringing. Once again he allowed me to approach the desk, and this time I forwarded every remaining line to my own extension so the ringing would stop.

It seemed eternity passed as we maintained our positions listening to his angry outbursts. He eventually saw the hallway sniper and began to taunt him as well, holding up his trigger device inviting the sniper to kill him so he would drop it and let the explosives go off. He would yell, "I could have been one of you – I took your BS test and could have been a cop myself" and similar insults. The front site remained steady. No response came from the well trained and disciplined professional behind it.

Dore's behavior was violent at times, sometimes cordial, then he would break out in laughter. But the entire time he was handling the Walther pistol in a very reckless manner. As he waved it around just four feet from the ladies, with the hammer pulled back and his finger on the trigger, I was concerned he would *accidently* shoot them.

I must have shown my anger at his handling of the gun, as he jumped up at one point aiming the gun at my head and yelling how I best stop looking mad. I raised my hands to show a surrendering posture as he yelled I had no right to be mad, and how he was the only one there with that right. I agreed with him, and worked to calm the situation with words. It worked and he settled back down.

After some time I realized that since he had jerked the line out of one phone, and I had forwarded all the others, there would be no way a hostage negotiator could contact him. So I fabricated another story designed to not only get the disabled phone back up, but to get me closer to his packs and weapon so I could see them closer and be prepared to describe them to law enforcement when we might escape.

I told him that the work comp folks had probably heard where he was by now, and maybe they were trying to call him. I told him he should let me return to the counter and repair the phone line he had ripped out so the work comp folks could call in. He allowed me to do so, then quickly ordered me back out again as soon as I had made the repair. As I returned to my post, I told the guard, "Extension 1907 is open."

He contacted the police command center with that information.

Not long after, the phone rang again. One of the ladies answered it, and I was quite relieved when she said, "Yes -- he's right here" and handed the phone to Dore. However, I became disappointed by the tone of Dore's voice. He was talking as if it were his best friend, mother or brother on the other end. We needed a professional police negotiator. My disappointment turned into irritation. I felt whoever this caller was, they were wasting critical time and I wanted this call to end so a skilled negotiator could get through. But about 10 minutes into the call, Dore backed his chair from blocking the door, opened it, and said, "Sure, I can let them go now."

I knew then that the professionalism of the negotiator on the other end of the line had even taken me by surprise.

The four of us wasted little time getting out of the building. As soon as the ladies stood up to go past him on their way out of the enclosure, the sniper in the hallway began moving into a more hostile position. His movement caught my eye, and it certainly kept Dore's attention as it looked like the sniper may shoot at any moment. At one point Dore turned back away from the sniper to look at us, and the sniper motioned aggressively for us to get out. As we moved out we were met by a swarm of officers and paramedics just out of sight from where we had just been held for so long.

It was 90 minutes after the hostage portion of his attack began, that we were released. I was put into an ambulance and rushed to the hospital (which was in lockdown until authorities could determine if there were others involved in our hostage situation) for observation. An investigator rode with me taking careful notes on the explosive pack material description, trigger device, firearm and any other observations I had made. I am certain the other three hostages were giving similar reports at the same time.

A little more than four hours after we were released he was talked into laying his gun down, and surrendering to authorities. The negotiator told him if he surrendered, he would go out the front door with an abundance of media filming him. However, if he forced them to kill him they would take his body out the back door and nobody would ever see it. That settled it -- he surrendered.

In the months that followed, the testimony of all involved resulted in his incarceration that will keep him off the streets for many years. This was his decision, confirmed by his own actions.

While nobody was physically hurt, one of his female hostages was left such a nervous wreck, that her hair thinned as if she had experienced chemotherapy. The last I knew, the prospects of ever holding any kind of a job looked quite bleak for her. The other receptionist continued working in the same capacity. The courageous and effective security guard went on to become the Security Director for a while, but has since gone into obscurity. I used the lessons learned to consult other organizations, and prepare this book on effective ministry emergency preparation. Such trauma hits different people different ways.

A small plaque hangs on the wall in the lobby beside the bullet-hole left by his only shot fired -- one that may have been an accidental discharge, or may have been done as mental preparation for a self-inflicted gunshot suicide. He fired that one shot after we were out.

Even after the arrest, Dore justified his actions. He told a Denver newspaper that he was injured because Focus on the Family (in his mind, a 108 million dollar a year organization that wouldn't help him feed his family) was to blame because they went with the low bid contractor who didn't use good safety practices. He went so far as to say what he did was insane, but what Focus did was worse.

THINK ABOUT IT:

- By taking notice of unrelated dangers a year earlier, Focus on the Family was better prepared when the gunman arrived.

- There was a VIP at Focus on the Family who had been engaged in dialogue with Dore prior to the incident. That person knew Dore was very angry, but just didn't think it would ever come to this. I learned of those conversations (and the individual's name) as I listened to Dore complain. But there was no restraining order, communication with police, or information shared with front desk people or those of us charged with the duty of being initial responders regarding any kind of official watch notice. An ineffective handful of people kept the information to themselves.

- Our only "tools" for directly dealing with the gunman were our presence and acumen. That was enough to keep the incident contained and managed, then to transition to law enforcement as soon as it was possible to do so. Had he started shooting before SWAT officers were in place, we were not prepared.

- Due to earlier training, everyone at Focus evacuated dutifully upon hearing the fire alarms. There was not a culture of "wait and see" -- they responded as trained.

- The quick thinking of initial responders kept others from entering the danger zone. Someone later mused, "knowing Dr. Dobson, he may have been compelled to go into the danger zone had he been in town." Our electrician (one of the initial responders who diverted evacuations from going through the crime scene) responded, "He [Dobson] wouldn't have got past me." That was a fact; it would have been a moment where an electrician outranked the President.

- One of our initial responders came into the scene a little too forcefully, running up to the counter and asking what was wrong. The startled gunman jumped up and put his gun to the responder's head yelling how he should just kill him right there. Those were very tense moments. Always approach unclear situations cautiously.

- You may know some of what an angry person feels about your ministry. You don't know everything that is being poured into their anger recipe until it cooks to boil, then becomes an investigation. I knew all about the accident. I saw the bone fragments on the rebar. I knew about the Worker's Compensation board ruling it as "horseplay." What I had not known about, was the hatred which had boiled for years, fueled by his "friends."

- We hadn't practiced most of what we did that day. We had simply identified a person to serve as security, decided in a larger scenario that this person would be supported by facilities staff, and had an automated alert system for pulling those resources together. Even without specific team training, that team made more good decisions than bad ones.

- Fabricating stories like I did is risky business in a tense situation. The more I have learned about criminal behavior in the years following that incident, the more I believe that was not the right way to handle any attacker. As hostage negotiators have told me since, always tell the truth. It was a mistake in strategy on my part that was covered by grace.

- We cannot underestimate the power of prayer that day. Many at Focus heard (via e-mail) from all over the world that people were praying. E-mail was still in its infancy in those days, and it was quite a remarkable experience to see how fast both the story and the prayer response were getting around.

- The investigation revealed it wasn't real wire between the trigger device and the military pack -- it was twisted string that looked like wire. In an adrenalin-induced state, important details can be missed or misread.

SCANDAL, CONTROVERSY, DECEPTIONS and ETHICS VIOLATIONS

I tracked all news stories related to ministries for a season attempting to see what the major concerns were. As I logged 2,000 news stories in a two year period, I compiled the categories and discovered scandal (controversy or ethics violations) to be the 4th most common on that list. So by 2006 I already knew scandal would be the 4th most likely reason our church or any others might make the news in a negative way.

As I was writing this section, my phone and e-mail communication with friends and family was largely centered on the questions of "what and why" as they knew of my security involvement with New Life Church. I began this section the first weekend of November, 2006 -- just two days after *it* happened to us. As it turned out, *it* was only the first of two major incidents New Life Church would face within a 14 month period.

Our Security Director called me on Thursday, November 2nd. As he began to recount what he knew, I had to pull over to compose myself. A story had just broken on a Denver radio station that our founding pastor was accused of soliciting sex, and that the male prostitute had furnished methamphetamines to him. Ted Haggard's secret was being rapidly exposed to us and the rest of the world simultaneously. I sat on the side of I -25 listening in disbelief to my cell phone conversation.

At first we all hoped it was a malicious fabrication, but as is often the case with such stories, illusions slowly gave way to disillusions.

I had often been concerned about Ted -- not due to any suspicion on my part, but what I recognize and say in other places of this book -- *if your ministry is on the move, there are weapons being fashioned against it*. I didn't see the arrow coming from this particular bush -- meth and gay sex -- by the senior pastor himself. As I began this section, we didn't know how it would end.

It was true.

One year after Dad passed away in 2005, my brothers and I, with our wives, spent the anniversary of his passing with Mom in Kansas. Early in the morning, on the anniversary of his death, I got up as I had often seen Dad do, went to his easy chair with a cup of coffee, turned on the light and opened his bible. I love to read the passages Dad had underlined. I don't know if the bookmarks were where Dad had left them or not, but that is where I read on that particular morning. One marker was in Proverbs where Dad had underlined *Pride goes before destruction and a haughty spirit before stumbling*[17].

I personally believe pride was the main issue with Ted. I know there are other things that lead to scandal, but pride often opens the gate wide -- not only towards scandal, but to other misbehaviors as well.

There was a personal e-mail exchange between Ted and I in 2004 where he explained how he had been delayed in getting back to me, as he was meeting in Tel Aviv with ... and went on to drop several prominent world leaders' names. An earlier e-mail to the general congregation (see inset) had similar tones of pride. I was struck by the sensationalism I was seeing and began to pray at that time that pride would not become a problem for him. Maybe those of us who were so struck should have done more than pray.

42

Ted often spoke of his ties to Washington and had become quite regular at dropping the names of famous people he had talked with. We all knew when he made TIME magazine's list of most influential evangelicals, and we often heard of things he had said to President Bush. But as the awful facts began to emerge concerning his misconduct, White House Deputy Press Secretary Tony Fratto issued a statement in answer to enquiries of just how influential Ted had been in the Bush Administration;

> Ted Haggard Nov 7, 2003 partial e-mail to the congregation (hint of pride?);
>
> "...Monday I was in the World Prayer Center and my cell phone rang. It was one of the special assistants to President Bush calling from the White House. It turns out that when the President was reviewing the list of those attending the signing of the partial birth abortion ban, he asked why I wasn't attending and asked that they call me. So the White House staff got onto the phones and were calling the NAE Washington office, our church office and my cell phone at the same time trying to see if I could come to the signing..."

He had been on a couple of calls, but was not a weekly participant in those calls. I believe he's been to the White House one or two times ... but there have been a lot of people who come to the White House. [18]

The world now knows the truth, and Ted Haggard was permanently removed as our home church pastor. The feelings from here were of intense sorrow, hurt, and disappointment. We were disillusioned – but that was a good thing. To be disillusioned indicates that there was an existing illusion to be corrected. Cut as it may (and this was like surgery), disillusionment corrects.

This book is not about *pride*, it's about alerting of, preparing for, and preventing tactics of the enemy. Pride is one of the most common and destructive weapons of his army. It is the assault rifle of the enemy's weapons -- seen often in the pictures of ministry casualties.

On Sunday November 5th, 2006, Ted and his wife Gayle were gone. They both wrote letters of goodbye to the church. Ted's letter was graciously accepted with nods from heads still reeling from disbelief. Gayle's letter was accepted with tears and a standing ovation. I cannot begin to express the feelings we all had during those difficult days. This storm was bigger than any safety or security ministry -- the entire church was aware of this one. I hope you never have to use their letters as a model in your ministry, but there are plenty of websites that still post both of them.

Ted's story continues. I wish him and Gayle the best in their journey.

THINK ABOUT IT:

- If you suspect pride is becoming an issue in your ministry, recognize it for what it is -- a developing attack strategy on your leadership -- and bring it to your leadership the same as you would report any other developing threat.

- New Life leadership took quick, decisive, significant and direct moves to remedy the indiscretion. That is perhaps the second most critical thing (taking a back seat only to God's grace) that saved our church from ruin.

- As with most exposed indiscretions, after it was over many recounted that there was something a little tilted with the way Ted ran things, and acknowledged he was unapproachable by any but a select few. Good leadership models include structured accountability, as well as being approachable. A lack of such may be a call for discussion as there could be a deeper underlying issue.

- If it feels wrong, pay attention. Intuition is a strong defense.

From accidents to violent crime to deceit, it is not easy to forecast what might happen at any given organization. One thing is certain, things will happen. The old model of disregarding any form of readiness in our faith-based organizations needs to change.

The dogmas of the quiet past are inadequate to the stormy present. The occasion is piled high with difficulty, and we must rise -- with the occasion. As our case is new, so we must think anew, and act anew.

Abraham Lincoln

CHAPTER 3
Balance

Eleven-year-old Cub Scout Brennan Hawkins was missing for four days in the rugged mountains of northeastern Utah in June of 2005. In our part of the country, we had been on the edge of our seats watching this search effort, partially because another young man missing from the same area a year earlier was never found. That other young man's dad was on the volunteer search team for Brennan. Little Brennan was found in fair condition by a volunteer rescue searcher. His mother was quoted as saying, "We are here to unequivocally tell you that the heavens are not closed. Prayers are answered and children come home."

While I am glad he was found, one detail of his story troubled me. One of the first things he told the rescuer who found him was that earlier he had seen guys (most likely rescue searchers) on horses, but he didn't know if they were good guys or bad so he had remained hiding as they rode by. It is awful to realize there may have been others lost in the past, who died without ever having been found, who may have experienced the same thing. As a culture we have convinced our kids that *most* people can't be trusted. That is simply wrong.

We cannot throw out all security concerns and tell our kids, "trust the world, it will be kind to you." I would never promote such a careless platform as that -- but I hope to illustrate the need for some pursuit of *balance*. Many find themselves not trusting anyone, and that is unfortunate.

There is an especially fine line to walk when it comes to balancing trust and security in a ministry. In military operations, errors on the side of security must be sometimes accepted as collateral damage. In a religious environment, error may be best on the side of compassion under grace. Security in a faith-based organization must be different than security in other cultures. Forgiveness is of higher value than condemnation but should not be exercised in a way that endangers others or compromises integrity.

That says easy. Walking through it can be a journey through fog.

When the active shooter entered New Life church on December 9th, 2007, under the influence of speed and anti-depressants, it was intense and quick. By the time Jeanne Assam stopped him with deadly force, he had already killed two young girls in our parking lot and two other young people earlier in the day at an Arvada, Colorado YWAM facility 77 miles to our north. There were others wounded by him at both sites. He had over 1,000 rounds of ammunition left when Jeanne stopped him.

> *My friend Jimmy Meeks is a 30+ year police veteran in Texas. With a heart towards security in churches, he has many great resources compiled on his website – www.safeatchurch.org.*

All three points of the deadly triangle were present – the gunman had the opportunity, intention and capacity to fulfill his discovered suicide promise of "Christian America – this is YOUR Columbine." There is no doubt he came to kill as many innocent people as he could before his own violent death, which was also part of his plan.

Some leaders don't want deadly force weapons in their organization and there are laws against such in some state or local jurisdictions. It is imperative to support those decisions and laws already in place. While I do believe tools of force, up to and including deadly force weapons, enhance the effectiveness of peacekeepers, it isn't guns or the lack thereof that determines if a ministry is safe or vulnerable. It is the effectiveness of the team and their plan.

That said, the fact remains that some attacks cannot be stopped with anything but a firearm.

I know one very devoted ministry security leader who is not afraid to pull off the road and engage inner city LA gangs and try to get them to change their ways. His wife and children do not ride with him when he is going through a seedy area because of his propensity to do this. He will walk right up to the most dangerous troublemakers (he calls them knuckleheads) and engage them. In one case I know of, he grabbed one of those tough guys by the head with both hands and made him look at him like an angry dad would do a 5-year-old and had a real *come to Jesus meeting* with him.

This man has a heart for his particular ministry (an evangelical Four-Square church). He doesn't carry any kind of a weapon, but he protects that particular church including the senior pastor very well in my opinion. One of the consequences of him having spent 22 years in prison is that he can't legally carry a weapon even if he wanted to. He wouldn't qualify as a security team member in many organizations who conduct any kind of a background check.

But if I am ever in another deadly force action in a ministry (Lord -- please not) he is one of the five men I would choose to have there with me. I would be quite confident to go into that stressful response situation with this man as my leader, beside or behind me.

Ministries come in a wide variety of flavors. There are churches, synagogues, charter-schools, colleges, counseling services, medical facilities, broadcasters, publishers, charitable outreaches, funeral homes and missions of many kinds. There are ministries devoted to agendas on all sides of every moral, theological, and social issue.

Of all such environments, houses of worship may pose the most challenging atmosphere for planning and implementing security measures. Houses of worship are dynamic congestions of crowds of various ages, child care, classrooms, public transportation, entertainment events, volunteer service, controversial and polarizing publicity, open cash handling, dignitary appearances / crowd interface, as well as daily office work. All of this activity is carried on with an open door to everyone -- especially those in need. The consistent schedule is often published for anyone to see.

> *You protect your flock because you love them! And when we are "under the influence" of love -- we are protective of others! In 1st Corinthians 13: Paul writes, "love...always protects..."(NIV). The good shepherd, Jesus said, will lay down his life for the sheep. We love our families, and we are committed to their protection. Why would we love our flocks any less?!...Jimmy Meeks*

In addition to the weekly programs, come all the human dynamic issues as well. Part of the business of church is helping members of the congregation and staff through emotional, mental, physical, financial, relational and criminal issues. Whether the particular activity is one of benevolence, marriage & family counseling, or addiction recovery, all such ministry comes with a certain risk factor.

To stop meeting those needs would be to stop being a church. To ignore the risks associated with those needs would be naive and reckless.

● ● ●

FOLLOW THE LEADER

Visionary leaders can be tough to follow. You must understand what they mean by every comment, and their passion may be mistaken as contradictive. I can only imagine how it was to walk with Christ. Consider the bewilderment Peter must have felt as he heard (and attempted to follow) a series of comments from Christ found in the 21st and 22nd chapters of Luke.

Peter first grasped that he should, "Be alert" (21:36). He then must have been glad to hear Jesus tell him to "Buy a sword" (22:36). I mean, what man in his right mind wouldn't want to hear his ministry leader encourage him to pick up a Glock at Cabela's? So Peter and another disciple bought swords (22:38). You could say that Peter was a charter member of the "Conceal Carry" crowd, and his permit was authorized by Jesus. Yet when he used it just 12 verses later, Jesus rebuked him. It makes it a bit easier to understand Peter's disillusionment shown seven verses later with the first of his famous three denials of Christ.

I am no theologian, so I make no attempt at revealing earth-shattering spiritual conclusions about this. But I do know weapons, and I understand authority. If you must ask if it is a good time to use deadly force -- it isn't. The use of deadly force is not the arena to proceed with the old "easier to get forgiveness than permission" approach. Yet that seems to be what Peter did (read Luke 22:49-50 carefully).

Jesus knew, and approved of the swords His men carried -- in fact He told them to obtain them. It was no oversight on His part that they had swords with them that night. But there must be good reason this is one of the few stories carried in all four Gospels. Perhaps it is good to consider it as a lesson learned regarding the careful, intentional, and accurate use of force by illustrating an improper use of force.

Many young peace keepers quickly say, "I would rather be judged by 12 than carried by 6." Fewer seasoned law enforcement officers say that so quick. There are reasons most law enforcement training focuses first on *when* to use deadly force, then *how* to use it.

In everything we do, we must be acutely aware of the primary mission of our particular ministry. It was not the safety plan that established the mission. It is not the ministry security personnel who lead the ministry mission. It is however, the duty of every department within the ministry to be knowledgeable and supportive of that mission. If there are people overly zealous in intense security, perhaps those folks may do better to serve elsewhere. A ministry doesn't exist for security, nor does any ministry owe its success to the security team.

The Ministry Safety team should consider the passage of scripture from 1 Corinthians 12:12-31 regarding the parts of the body. Parts of the body that are most applicable to our team would be the eyes, ears, and palm of the hands. If anyone on your team resembles the trigger finger, you should probably ask that person to step off the team. Better yet -- be careful to never recruit such people in the first place.

Safety and security planning is like storm preparation. Just because you may be well prepared for a storm at your home, doesn't mean you are a storm preparation agency. It is still your home, with all your personal family plans -- clothes for the kids, groceries for the fridge, and a nice bed for rest -- it's not storm central. Planning for a storm (while important) is only incidental to the success of your home.

The driving force of many faith-based organizations is compassion. Pure selfless compassion is the best defense against any form of hatred, which is the driving force of most acts of violence. In the last chapter of this book you will read about two extraordinary men who cleared dozens of children out of the hallway at New Life Church as bullets narrowly missed them. As soon as the children were cleared, both of those unarmed defenders ran to their vehicles for pistols they had, but were not yet authorized to carry in their security duties.

Both had just witnessed firsthand the horror of the active shooter walking in with deadly intent and action. As one of those men was reaching for his pistol in his vehicle, he heard us report over radio that the shooter was down. With no hesitation, his hand then went to his medical bag instead of his weapon in hopes he might be able to save any who may have been hurt by the shooter. If there is a model of the character of a ministry security agent, it will reflect that ability to quickly default to the compassionate nature even in the worst of situations.

• • •

Recent *hate crime* legislation is of debatable value. Most violence against persons or groups *is* hate based, and to try and define only crimes against certain lifestyles or cultures as hatred based appears agenda driven and politically motivated. My complaint is not based on those that *are* categorized as hate crimes -- rather those which *are not.*

When Larry Gene Ashbrook shouted anti-Christian venom as he gunned down fourteen (seven of whom died) in the Ft. Worth Wedgewood Baptist Church on 9/15/1999 (one of the three worst church shootings in U.S. history) the attack was not categorized as a "hate crime." Yet when Jim David Adkisson killed two in a Knoxville, Tennessee Unitarian church and later admitted obstinate disparity with one of that church's opinions on a particular social issue, it was quickly categorized as a hate crime (as it should have been).

The most violent attack in a U.S. school was the bombing of the Bath Michigan Consolidated School on May 18th, 1927. School Board member Andrew Kehoe became enraged over property tax issues and the pending foreclosure of his own property. He rigged explosives that killed 45 (most were children 7-12 years old) and wounded 58. Yet by the definition of today's "hate crimes" that attack would not qualify.

Hatred stinks, no matter what group, individual or cause it is directed towards. Ministry security should interrupt hatred, while representing their ministry.

We should embrace biblical teachings to "not worry about your life, what you will eat or drink, or about your body, what you will wear..."[19] Being confident in faith doesn't mean we stop participation in our own preservation and social interaction. We trust God for provision, but we don't sit up in bed in the morning and raise our hands for clothes to float down on us out of heaven. We don't stroll leisurely through the day with a heavenly mist occasionally sprayed into our mouths to keep us hydrated in between tasty morsels of surprise that find themselves lodged in our teeth, satisfying our hunger. Even the Israelites had to gather the manna that appeared every day.

The procurement and administration of those needs is an intentional process of action on our part. We should consider safety and security in a similar fashion.

Yet very few faith-based organizations are intentional about security. This is especially true of churches. Many still say, "God will provide." He does, but He expects a little participation. The people in our care and the amenities they have funded with their contributions are worthy of security considerations.

Ministry leadership should accept responsibility of protection out of concern for their staff, visitors and congregants. But if they remain unmoved by that, there is the black & white issue of regulatory compliance. While I would not recommend beating them over the head with a code book, every organization should be fully aware of the duties of compliance.

• • •

Compliance with authority (not fun reading, but good to know).

There are federal obligations under the Occupational Safety and Health Act (OSH Act) of 1970 to provide for intentional safety of staff. There are also often local level life safety codes to protect everyone (employees, volunteers and visitors) using a ministry's buildings, campus and vehicles.

The bottom line of the consolidation of all such code considerations is that most employers and / or building operators are required to have an Emergency Action Plan (EAP), aka Emergency Operations Plan, Safety / Security Plan, or similar terms. Compliance with a required

EAP is a great start for a ministry safety plan, but keep it simple and don't read more into code compliance than what is applicable.

If fire extinguishers are required or provided in your workplace, and if anyone will be evacuating during a fire or other emergency, then OSH Act's 29 CFR (Code of Federal Regulations) 1910.157 requires that employer to have an EAP[20].

Furthermore, section 5(a)(1) of the OSH Act states that every employer in the United States *shall furnish to each of his employees employment and a place of employment which are free from recognized hazards that are causing or are likely to cause death or serious physical harm to his employees.*

That phrase is considered the "catch-all" mandate to cover anything else not specifically detailed by line item in the CFR. It is widely known as the *General Duty Clause* of the OSH Act. It is not specific to any trade (such as construction or shipbuilding), it is specific to *employers*. The OSH Act would be applicable to *employees* of a church but not applicable to guests.

The Occupational Safety and Health Administration (OSHA) is the federal *authority having jurisdiction* (AHJ) which sets and enforces protective workplace safety and health standards as they are detailed in the OSH Act. OSHA also provides information, training, and assistance to employers and workers. Compliance with the OSH Act is driven by investigation, litigation and fines administered by OSHA.

If there is an injury accident involving an employee, OSHA may investigate. If OSHA receives a letter of complaint from a current or past employee, the employer will either hear from OSHA or enjoy their company -- either way there will be a response required of the employer which documents evidence of safety training and awareness. If a staff member is killed while on duty, OSHA will investigate.

OSHA typically comes in only after an incident. They rarely check employers' compliance with the legal obligation. But any investigation will focus on the employer's documented evidence of safety awareness and actions before and during the incident.

The OSH Act is not the only compliance code to be aware of. While OSHA is driven by after-the fact litigation and inspections, other codes are driven by different requirements and processes.

Those other codes are typically local level requirements, enforced by local AHJs. Most commonly such regulations are specified in municipal codes, and enforced by local agencies. The compliance of employers and building owners are confirmed through certifications, permits, licensing, and inspections by code enforcement agents of those local level codes. Depending on the regulatory profile of any territory, the enforcement agents may be from offices of police, code enforcement, fire departments, building officials or any combination of these or others.

A common local AHJ is the fire department. Code enforcement may fall under a sub-category known as fire prevention or similar titles. The code most commonly enforced is the International Fire Code (IFC). Although that code is updated every three years (there is or will be an IFC 2012, 2015, 2018 etc.) local jurisdictional adoption typically lags for years behind those releases. It is common to find a particular jurisdiction still enforcing a 10-year-old code release. 1997 and 2003 were both major revision code improvements (following the OKC bombing and the 9/11 attacks). Jurisdictions often adopt major revision dates more quickly.

At the time of this writing, it is safe to say that many jurisdictions are still enforcing IFC 2003, so the following comments are based on that code release.

While a typical EAP may be primarily *fire code* related, it should be much more than a *fire* safety plan. Fire Code is the most clearly defined mandate a ministry EAP measures up to, so it serves as a common sense starting point for a good plan. There are some significant qualifiers regarding fire code compliance to understand:

- Not all jurisdictions mandate IFC. Some mandate the Uniform Fire Code (UFC), National Fire Protection Association (NFPA), other codes or none.

- Those who do mandate IFC may mandate a different year than 2003 (and of course as years pass, other versions will become more prevalent).

- Many metropolitan areas have *supplemental edits* that are adopted by local authorities to supplement some sections of a code (Requirement for "occupant-use hose stations" is often stricken from the IFC for local adaptation as one example).

- Codes vary in applicability by building use (occupancy type) and size (occupancy load). IFC 2003 section 404.2.1 does not require churches (type "A" occupancies) of under a 2,000 person "occupant load" to have an EAP (unless there is a mezzanine in a type A area – then any size of church must have an EAP). But here again, many local jurisdictions are inclined to strike that exception and require that *any* type A occupancy have a plan.

Whether technically *required* by code or not, it is a safe matter of prudence to voluntarily apply a relative code for the safety of a ministry's staff, volunteers, and visitors.

You should verify what (if any) fire or life safety codes your church or ministry is required (or voluntarily chooses) to be compliant with and make certain your programs meet the requirements. In the case of compliance under IFC 2003, you may be required to submit your comprehensive plan for approval (even without an incident) unless local supplements have stricken that evidence requirement.

Life Safety floor plans are an important part of plans. Important things (as required by International Fire Code 2003 section 403) to have on those floor plans are:

- Occupancy assembly point(s).

- Locations of fire hydrants.

- Normal routes of fire department vehicle access.

- Accessible Exits and egress routes. (Primary and secondary egress routes are required).

- Areas of refuge inside the building for *"Shelter in Place."*

- Manual fire alarm pull-stations.

- Portable fire extinguishers.

- Occupant-use hose stations (sometimes excluded by local jurisdictions – check with your Fire Prevention Office first).

- Location(s) of fire alarm annunciator panels and controls.

● ● ●

As much as there are letter-of-the-law requirements to be aware of, if we accept responsibility for safety and security we can move forward in the spirit-of-the-law.

No individual or team -- regardless of training, strength, degrees, licenses or certifications -- can guarantee security. The definition of secure, "free from danger or risk of loss" is not possible at all with simple human planning. Any serious plan, system, team, or response should recognize and participate in the foundational necessity of faith. It is on this spirit of humble recognition that we should build any plan.

That said, there is still a seasoned and determined enemy at the gate.

No weapon forged against you will prevail (Isaiah 54:17 NIV).

Shrewd leaders recognize there is a tenacious enemy opposed to their mission. Consistent with the very nature of warfare, if an organization is on the move, there are weapons being fashioned and plans being made for an attack by that enemy. This is not a call for fear, but rather a rational reminder of a very real, active and determined enemy. The security and safety of everyone associated with churches and faith-based organizations requires people, parts and processes that are intentionally focused on protection.

To prepare at all is to be a lot further down the path of readiness than many churches and ministries have ever dared to go. Codes intimidate some organizations so they don't even try, deciding instead to take their chances should some investigation occur. Codes are not as difficult to satisfy as often thought. When that investigator drops by your church offices, if he sees IFC 2003, OSHA CFR 29, and your Emergency Action Plan together in your book shelf, his visit will begin as one of unusual and pleasant surprise. Of course I hope *Evil Invades Sanctuary* is right there on your bookshelf with them.

A good safety plan supports and never distracts from the ministry purpose. The plan supports the ministry mission, welcoming those that the particular ministry is designed to reach, while keeping their safety in mind if threats or hazards are encountered.

Though we cannot *assure* safety, we should *pursue* safety as a priority and commit to stand with the innocent when trouble comes through the doors. The word "safety" is used very specifically. There will be volunteers serving here. Safety includes *security*, but to call the overall plan *security* may send a message of fear, draw criticism for misplaced priorities, or create sensationalism. The call to serve in a *safety ministry* accurately reflects the culture and motivates the compassionate side of our nature, while a call to serve in "security" may pull more on the sensational nature. In a faith-based culture, we need people motivated by compassion.

Those volunteers will have inconsistent availability and the ministry they serve is dynamic. Somewhere between "nothing" and "ideal", your safety plan will come around. At first the Incident Commander may also be the one who shuts off the fire alarm. The person you may recommend to accompany funds transported to the bank each week may actually be the head usher or CFO. You may not have enough (or any) law enforcement volunteers to serve as trained security. These appointments may be a reliable grocery clerk or farmer. As you grow, more volunteers will come to the aid of those serving.

Start by initiating a "**Ministry Safety Team**" (MST), with someone designated as the MST Manager. It will resemble the same model used by other churches, where the primary duty is to manage and facilitate the "**Church Safety Plan**." This team, and their awareness of the needs, is the single most important thing to be done. This team will manage and improve the plan.

You may start with two volunteers. Have them recommend safety program ideas and keep the ball rolling. From that small beginning, allow the team to assemble. They may become a small group ministry as they develop effective plans.

No plan, regardless of attention to detail, will ever answer every possible scenario. The question emergency planners often hear is "what do you do with a fire evacuation during a lightning storm?"

You punt.

Emergency planning is a lot like a football huddle. You make the plan, decide who goes where, who blocks where, and how to run down which sideline. But as soon as the ball is snapped, the field changes from how you envisioned in the huddle. The players, leadership, and procedures on your team should be effective enough to move towards the goal of safety by dynamically reading the play and each other, being constantly aware of the lay of the field, their individual player strengths and weaknesses, and the capacity and historical tactics of the opposition.

I also heard a speaker at a U.S. military symposium describe major incident response as being more like jazz than a symphony.

In a symphony, the musical piece is very carefully and rigidly choreographed and structured. Each player follows the sheet music and conductor to strike exactly the correct note at precisely the right time with the perfect effort and volume.

In Jazz, one leads and others join in -- sometimes one at a time -- until a rhythm and sound emerge that flows in tempo. Jazz pieces are, by nature of their style, never played exactly alike in any two performances. Done well, they produce a very moving and enjoyable experience.

Security operations in any environment are dynamic. Having no plan is reckless, but over planning is not good either. Somewhere in between is a good model.

Develop your game plan (performance) with a vision of success. The return to normalcy is central to all security planning -- be focused on that vision. As a good southern pastor said about *vision*;

"If you don't see it before you see it, you'll never see it."[21]

CHAPTER 4
Options of Readiness

Regardless of cultural, regional, or other factors unique to each organization there are three critical elements of incident readiness:

1. PEOPLE -- The people who plan and execute the program.

2. PARTS -- The tools they use and manage to operate a safe and secure environment.

3. PROCESSES -- The procedures they go by.

Consider concepts in this chapter as *options* because the details vary with each organization. Laws governing ministry environment safety and security operations vary from one jurisdiction to another. The risks associated with a metropolitan Orthodox church in downtown Miami, Florida are much different than the risks associated with a rural Baptist church outside of Trapper Creek, Alaska. The culture between the two is equally different. A church program is going to vary from a program for a charter school.

The concepts offered as options intend to show how other models have worked -- not to lay down a strict how-to. Even the name of each program should be titled to fit the ministry in which it operates.

● ● ●

THE PEOPLE

Safety and security activities may have been incidental roles filled by capable and dedicated people within some faith-based organizations for years. As ministries grow and risks increase, those roles should become intentional and defined. That doesn't mean every ministry needs a full-time security director. In fact, that is impractical for most. But whoever fills the role, be it a faithful volunteer who also mows the grass, or a dedicated team, they should be intentional about safety and security, giving sincere consideration to, "what to do if…"

It is important to understand terminologies of the emergency response business. A first responder indicates one with an agency issued license to be a uniformed public servant. First responders are fire fighters, law enforcement officers and emergency medical professionals. An *initial responder* (or *front-line responder* as labeled by the Department of Homeland Security) is a site staff or volunteer person designated within any organization to be an immediate emergency responder.

One purpose of this section is to identify key positions of initial responders. It is not an attempt to micro-define their operational roles. To maintain a simple and optional theme, suggestions are offered to start the program. There is no substitute for time, experience and study to bring definition to those developing programs. The intended result is an effective program managed by folks who genuinely represent the specific ministry. It is no accident that the bulk of this chapter is on the people. The people you choose will work through the parts and process needed to make your plan an effective one.

Using a model title of Ministry Safety Team (MST), one person may serve some or all of these functions in smaller churches. Options for a model MST are:

Ministry Safety Team Leadership (MSTL)

Traditional Response Team (TRT)

Medical Response Team (MRT)

Professional Protection Team (PPT)

An organizational chart for this MST may look like this;

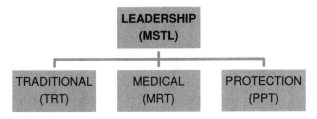

TEAM CONCEPTS and DESCRIPTIONS

Ministry Safety Team Leadership (MSTL)

Leadership can be made up of each of the sub-team leaders and the primary person identified by the ministry as responsible for the program.

Whether it is the pastor of a small church, volunteer caretaker, or the chief safety officer of a structured department of an international ministry, someone should be designated as the overall program's primary leader. If it is a volunteer position, consider making their leadership appointment a limited term. It may beneficial for them to know going in that it is not a life-long appointment, and the day may come to let another lead for a season.

The department overseeing the safety / security program varies from one ministry to the next. It often comes down to competencies or passions of a particular person more than a decision based on logical and standard departmental affiliations. I see safety / security programs most commonly overseen by the Facilities or HR departments, either of which would earn my highest recommendation if a ministry had no other prevailing factors. I have also seen safety / security fall under the Financial (risk management) office, as a direct report to the ministry executive, and even occasionally as a function of the IT department.

In early developmental stages of the program, the MSTL may need to meet often. As the program stabilizes and matures, this team will need to come together for planning sessions less often. But there will always be good reasons to maintain the MSTL. Occasional situations and reviews may be best managed by this group.

Traditional Response Team (TRT)

When developing a program avoid re-inventing as much of the wheel as possible. There are people already in place in any organization who are familiar with the dynamics of the ministry; use them. Large organizations have specific *operations* (aka facilities, maintenance, custodial or housekeeping) departments. In smaller churches and ministries such roles may simply be additional responsibilities of other positions. Just about every church has ushers and / or greeters.

These are the first people to consider in the development of the TRT. This is the operations staff common to most organizations and / or ushers and greeters common to almost any church. A Para-church ministry may not have ushers, but will have some sort of operational staff. Since these functions are commonly already in place and familiar with the facility and people, they are a common sense starting point.

Many or all of those folks can be trained or cross-trained as initial responders. If a ministry is large enough to have a specific safety team, these traditional roles should still be formally connected to that team.

In small churches or in regular work weeks and small events of larger churches, common facilities staff may serve safety duties without specific medical or security teams present. There is nothing at all wrong with having these traditional common roles function as the entire Ministry Safety Team in many situations.

However when ministry populations swell significantly for big church events, common duties such as cleaning, maintenance, and event set-up are increased as well. In such events, these folks may already be stretched thin before emergencies, so they may not be the best eyes and ears for incident prevention and response. Therefore in bigger church environments, additional resources (specifically medical and security) are encouraged for the swollen population times.

There are many incidents that may involve the TRT. Lost children, fire alarms, utility interruptions, or any emergency that will require civil first responders are examples of when at least some of the operational staff and / or ushers may naturally put on an initial responder hat.

Don't overlook the potential for discovering relative initial responder skills within the regular church staff. In any organization there may be a secretary who was previously a nurse. She may be interested in serving medically when an incident occurs. A night-time custodian may be going to school during the day studying criminal justice in pursuit of a law enforcement career. Find them and consider their service.

One of the most important people to have an intentional connection with is the front desk receptionist or others who serve in a similar capacity. They typically know everyone who belongs in the building and those who don't. By nature of their position they are a front-line responder and / or target; all the more reason they are a natural and critical contact. In churches with bookstores, other "points of sale", or benevolence stations, those persons should have a direct connection with the MST, and are good eyes and ears for suspicious behavior.

FACILITIES / OPERATIONS

Very small churches and those who rent facilities from others only for events may not have operations or facilities staff. But for those who do, this group should be a key part of the MST.

I can imagine some of my security colleagues groaning, gnashing their teeth and tearing their clothes at this, but I believe an operations department leader (supervisor, manager or director of maintenance, facilities or hospitality as the case may be) is a great consideration to lead the entire Ministry Safety Team. Especially in times of tighter budgets, a facilities manager is often the right choice for safety and security leadership. But it should be an intentional decision affirmed by ministry leadership and reinforced with training.

These folks know which keys open which doors, where the primary utility service entries are, and what electrical circuits support which equipment, power outlets and lights. They know how the building fire alarm and suppression systems work, which areas of the parking lot get the most ice in the winter, and where the roof access is. They know where the building blueprints and specifications are and how to read them (well -- they should). In a smaller church, this "team" may simply be an additional activity of the pastor, or the church member who built the church -- but nonetheless, somebody knows where all this stuff is and how to use it. The rest of the staff and congregants may think this person or department only knows where extra toilet paper is kept, but nobody knows the building as well as these folks. Like the front receptionist, they know everyone in the building.

If it is a rented facility the contact information for the landlord's maintenance contacts should be in some form of a readily available and current roster. Other churches may not have a facilities staff per se, and maintenance duties of mowing grass, servicing furnaces and patching the roof (in owner-occupied facilities) passes from one volunteer, elder or usher to another.

But whoever serves in such functions should have a part in the safety / security operations.

USHERS / GREETERS / PARKING ATTENDANTS

If the ministry is a church, this is the other critical part of the TRT. Again, whether it's a small church or one large enough to have many ushers, greeters and parking attendants, these folks will naturally (to some degree) serve an important role in crisis situations. As said regarding facilities managers, there is nothing wrong with smaller churches having an usher designated to lead the MST (again, being authorized and trained to do so).

So once again, I sense that some of my colleagues may have just thrown this book across the room as they race to their computers to blog on the audacity of such a suggestion. But to have ushers and greeters serve as the safety and security team may be all some churches can do. If so, that is how they should handle it.

When a crisis erupts, ushers and greeters who are so trained and have some forethought of expectation are much better prepared to lead through it. If they've been assigned roles specific to emergency response, they will operate with confidence in crowd control. That confidence itself can potentially lessen chaos and panic, mitigate the likelihood of injury, facilitate an effective transition to civil first responders and accelerate the return to normalcy.

> Former U.S. Marshall Tina Lewis Rowe provides a great manual for using such folks. Her website is www.tinalewisrowe.com. There are numerous church security related materials she offers for the asking. I most encourage you to get the one entitled, "The Role of Ushers and Greeters in Church Security."

Some large churches have parking facilities and driveways laid out well enough there is no need for parking attendants. There are also small churches where parking attendants are an important part of the culture. If there are parking attendants they should have an intentional link to the MST. Whether considering a lost child, first responder vehicle guidance, license plates on a watch list or outer perimeter defense – these folks can be crucial to the program.

There may be some in each of these resource pools (facilities, ushers, greeters) that slip to various other roles in times of crisis. If an usher is a doctor, he or she may naturally serve in a medical capacity if an injury occurs. Empower people to serve consistent with their gifting, interests and / or experience.

Medical Response Team (MRT)

The next group to consider is the Medical Response Team. Names such as Emergency Medical Team (that would eventually be called the EMT) should be avoided due to their similarity to first responder names (i.e. Emergency Medical Technician). Avoid confusion by choosing descriptive terms that can be easily remembered, but not confused with others.

MRT members are often congregants or staff who worship or work in otherwise normal ways until an incident occurs. By having them signed up prior to an incident, they can quickly become a medical responder when needed.

Assuming the volunteer model, most of the MRT will already have training and certifications through their regular employment. Many in the medical field carry pagers or cell phones with them at all times. There is no need to complicate their lives by having them adjust to the other MST communications standards. Consider letting MRT folks keep their familiar communication tools if they have them.

Once they have agreed to MRT participation, their contact information should be available for quick reference when needed. Just as ushers have reserved seating close to church aisles, so can active MRT members. If the MRT member is an employee (Para-church ministry or work week office settings in a church) their normal location may be their desk in accounting, correspondence, or whatever department they happen to work in – but make certain their contact info is available to all involved with emergency response duties.

> Every organization should have an ample distribution of automated external defibrillators or AEDs. No part of a building should be more than 60 seconds away from an AED at a normal walk. Medical professionals are often willing to donate these to their home church.

Some churches or ministries may not have anyone with medical careers or training. In these cases other trainable folks may be assigned to such roles. Women who raised children understand some degree of medical procedures. Many who participated in sports understand injury treatment in some way. There are other options outside of trained and certified medical professionals. If such people are the right choices to serve in this capacity get them certified in *child and adult CPR*, *Medical First Aid* and *AED* by the Red Cross, American Heart Association or other common resources.

Unfortunate as it is, there are people inclined to sue a ministry. Historically, many of those lawsuits were brought by ministry staff or volunteers (or even disgruntled pastors). Therefore it is important that all MST members (and especially the MRT and PPT) be aware of local laws and function with shrewdness. We never know (whether rendering assistance to a stranger or employee) if there may be a hidden motive. Good Samaritan laws help reduce the risk, but creative lawyers and motivated plaintiffs can be dangerous.

I am aware of a child who was injured by a poorly maintained door. The parents were very involved in the church and not inclined towards litigation. However, by the time that child turned 18 he had gone his own way and didn't care for the church. He had some remaining physical evidence of the injury, so successfully sued the church as an adult. He was no longer held to his parents' decision of not pursuing litigation when he was a child.

Don't operate in fear of lawsuits; just be mindful in training, responses and documentation. A lawsuit claiming negligence (i.e. no safety program) is more likely to be successful than one claiming an ineffective program. Put a plan in place mindful of applicable laws, but get started.

For some ministries and churches, having traditional team support for emergencies and a defined medical response group is all the further they wish to go. While I personally encourage all to go to the next step (security), to have just these first two levels is much better than nothing. And they are the two most crucial concerns for most ministry environments – a good place to start and a priority to maintain.

For those ministries and churches that can merge security into their program I encourage them to do so. Following are options for security specific operations.

Professional Protection Team (PPT)

These defensive men and women protect people and property. Individual PPT assignments may cover many bases (in a large church these may be specific sub-teams and in smaller environments one person may serve every role). They may include;

- Team Leader

- Executive Protection

- Inside Patrol

- Outside Patrol

Team Leader

A position assigned to lead during events, and aware of team assignments of all the MST. In the case of a major incident in a large environment, this position may participate in an incident command structure.

Incidents managed by a team leader could be anything from minor inconveniences up to a deadly force incident. PPT leaders manage incidents based on what is developing in front of them and maintain good communication interface with other MST members. Those assigned to lead protection activities should be aware of "chargeable offenses." The team leader should be able to navigate incidents with legal ramifications in mind (for all the same reasons the medical team should be judicious in respect to legal concerns). This leader may ideally be someone with law enforcement, military or private security training but don't discount others who are responsible and trainable with representative leadership abilities.

Executive Protection (EP)

A role typically assigned to the senior pastor, primary speaker or ministry executive. An EP might travel or move with them (shoulder position), and / or sit in a strategic assignment (jump seat) in assembly environments.

> *"And David put him in charge of his body-guard" ... 2 Samuel 23:23 (speaking of Benaiah – one of David's mighty men)*
>
> An old testament EP

A great resource specifically on the subject of Executive Protection is Robert L. Oatman's trilogy on Executive Protection. While secular in nature, the protection principles are applicable to many things we experience in ministries. If executives travel a lot, security is a concern in those travels and these books are a must for the ministry team assigned to executives. The three books are:

1.   The Art of Executive Protection (Baltimore, MD: Noble House, 1997)

2.   Executive Protection: New Solutions for a New Era (Baltimore, MD: Noble House, 2006)

3.   Executive Protection: Rising to the Challenge (ASIS International, 2009)

Larger organizations may also consider sending EPs to Oatman's training programs in Baltimore. Information is available at www.rloatman.com.

Call the person to be protected what you want -- executive, VIP, package -- the code tag (used in all communications) indicates a specific personal target of opportunity. Often the individual being protected is known as the "charge." If there is more than one charge, assignments should be clear to everyone involved (including the charge) prior to the event.

Inside Patrol

This could be one or more who roam the building(s) to discover and manage developing threats or potential hazards. In a church service, there are times when the halls are filled with many people. Once services have begun however, there is rarely any need for those not serving specific functions to be in the children's area, church offices, or other non-assembly areas.

It is a matter of simple due diligence to conduct intentional checks of those areas to guard against the many mischievous acts that occur while others are gathered in the worship service.

Some inside patrol should be assigned to specific placements throughout the sanctuary as well. These seated members can be with their families, and should not be obviously looking around (which itself is a service disruption). These positions should be acutely aware of all activity going on around them, the platform, behind the platform, windows, doors, aisles and any specific areas of vulnerability within their strategically selected views.

Some should remain close to each primary building entrance.

Outside Patrol

Perimeter security concepts seen in government, military and private sectors apply to ministries as well. Most serious church crimes happen outside in the parking lot or on the grounds. Crimes of deadly force (as one example) occur outside of the buildings at a rate of nearly 2-to-1 compared to the inside in hundreds of such stories tracked. Lesser crimes and mischievousness are just as prominent in the outside environment. There have been very few child abductions from inside a church; the overwhelming majority occurred in parking lots and playgrounds.

Even in the case of crimes that happen inside the building, the perpetrator arrives from and leaves to the outside. The more known or observed about a threat potential outside, the better that threat is managed, and fewer people are exposed to the danger. The outside team is often the first eyes on a developing incident or active in identification or recovery as an offender leaves the property.

In order to effectively respond in an emergency, the outside person or team should know significant details of the building exterior, outside equipment, parking lot and drive patterns. They should develop extensive familiarity with the layout, traffic patterns, and potential problems. Details such as the quantity of regular and handicap parking spaces, hiding places, typical first responder routes, exterior equipment condition and environmental vulnerabilities should be as well known to them as if it were their home so they know when anything has changed.

Some level of security representation should be designated for the outside. If a ministry only has two security people, one should focus on the exterior. Ratios go higher towards the inside as resources grow, but always keep some of the team focused on the exterior.

INCIDENT COMMAND

While there is no need to show it as a position in the organization chart, in the case of a large scale incident, team leaders may need to assemble as an

FEMA offers no-cost online training for incident commanders. Information on ICS (Incident Command Systems) can be found at http://training.fema.gov/EMIWeb/IS/ICSResource/index.htm.

incident command center, where they make joint decisions or participate in a unified command structure with civil first responders.

Incident command operations change with the nature of the incident. Some may need to have the senior pastor or ministry executive to participate in command center activities. Other situations may not require their presence, but could use a public information or HR representative designated by the ministry.

A person familiar with incident command operations is crucial when such a group is needed. Many skill sets are applicable to incident command. A person that coordinates any kind of dynamic environment might be a good recruit for such a position as Incident Commander. There are dozens of examples of such folks with multi-task and coordination abilities that can be considered for such a position -- you may need to think outside the box a little.

You may choose to have some folks named and ready specifically to serve in such a capacity. In a major scale incident, the leaders of the other teams may be in a command center, but they are going to be very focused on their specific responsibilities. The team leaders are *heads down* on their specific concerns while the Incident Commander is *heads up* looking across all current activities as well as developing issues beyond the immediate scene.

VOLUNTEERS

Our nation's baby boomers are retiring from their careers en masse. In President Bush's state of the Union address in January 2002, the 9/11 attacks were still fresh on our minds, and security mindsets were still popular. President Bush asked every American to "commit at least two years, 4,000 hours over the rest of your lifetime, to the service of your neighbors and your nation." This request combined with the retiring professional population presents a great potential volunteer network. Many of these potential volunteers were professionals in fields of law enforcement, military, medical, facilities, safety or security -- all of which are prime resource pools for the skills needed for ministry safety teams.

Be careful however of considering only people from these backgrounds. Conversations about credentials are often driven by pride, competition or exclusivity. While it is often best to draw from credentialed pools, remember that decisions of whether to call the qualified or qualify the called are over our pay scale. If there are those who feel called to serve in this capacity, don't rule them out just because of a lack of related employment history or credentials. While they should meet moral qualifications and exhibit relative aptitude, the best team members (or even leaders) may have never operated in an official facilities, medical or protection capacity before. Financial, educational, construction, utilities, communication, travel / tourism, transportation and retail sectors have all experienced increased safety and security concerns in recent years. As a result there are many good resources from pools such as these.

Well trained and seasoned veterans are a great resource, if they can work well in a ministry environment. That can be an issue. A ministry is not a hospital, military operation or police precinct. Ministry volunteers are seldom motivated by the same structural hierarchy that troops and officers have responded to in uniformed structures. Some who have spent their lives in those disciplined chain-of-command careers have trouble with the concepts of grace and ministry, and aspects of faith-based and mission-driven management.

Of course ministry safety leaders and team members with military, law enforcement, security, medical or other credentialed experience with a heart to support ministry leadership are still excellent considerations. Many do have the character to motivate volunteers, the discernment to separate real issues from annoyances, and an ability to lead in a way conducive to the culture.

Use caution with ministry security team participation by any who are dogmatic about gun rights, martial arts, or similar issues. For those who didn't throw the book and are still reading, allow me to explain.

When it comes to determining the appropriate use of force in response to incidents, you do not want anyone with dogmas of any kind that could cloud their judgment. Besides obvious concerns regarding excessive force injury, there are other consequences too.

Whether justified or not, extreme and relentless scrutiny can be expected following any significant use of force. Segments of society oppose private ownership of firearms, any form of protective action or abhor faith-based ministries. Count on it that such folks will cause as much trouble as possible, with all the media attention they can muster to bring down the ministry. For the same reasons law enforcement agencies steer away from radical employees, so should ministries.

Ministries are responsible for the actions of their appointed representatives. If an incident occurs at a ministry where an appointed security individual was instrumental in mitigating a threat by using force, count on extreme scrutiny from media, attorneys for the offender, the general public and even the congregation.

For example, let's say a person is outspoken on the right to defend ourselves with firearms and has been active and zealous in second amendment rights protection. Perhaps they have written letters to the local editor, staged protests against gun restriction legislation, or in similar ways expressed bold passion in support of such issues. They have left a trail of published and witnessed fuel for litigation.

Such zeal is sufficient cause for pause in considering them to represent a ministry in protective actions. When a ministry appoints agents of protection, they are essentially making a statement that, "We are here for the hurting. But if we cannot help them and they become a threat, we are authorizing you to intervene with appropriate means up to and including the use of deadly force if needed." If an attack was stopped with the use of such force by the character referred to in this example, the liability risk for the ministry is exponentially higher.

> Consider Verbal Judo and other de-escalation techniques a high training priority. Ask local law enforcement where such training is available in your area. If you are forced to use deadly force in your ministry, you don't want an opposing attorney showing the jury you had *nothing but* deadly force training.

Regardless of the cautions expressed, it is good to consider volunteers for a safety program. As ministry security becomes more accepted, but operating budgets remain tight, the need for volunteer professionals grows. There is simply more to do in establishing effective safety than typical existing staff has the time, expertise, or in some cases even the desire to deal with. Volunteers are especially effective in a church environment where the occupancy load swells significantly for five to 10 hours each week for weekend service and / or special events. It makes good sense to support such occupancy increases with volunteers.

For larger organizations, a specific volunteer coordinator should be considered. Such a position can be easily justified by documenting accomplishments and total hours of all (not just those serving in safety / security roles) ministry volunteers coordinated by the position. In addition to having a well-run volunteer program, the volunteers themselves get the tax benefits of having certain portions (vehicle mileage and duty-related expenses) verified by the ministry. There isn't much pay in the volunteer business, so a little appreciation by helping them at tax time goes a long way. Law enforcement agencies, large charities and educational institutions often have staff volunteer coordinators willing to share details of those positions if asked.

It is imperative to maintain good coordination and communication between employees and volunteers. Ministry staff involvement with the security / safety volunteers is critical. Of 168 hours in every week, volunteers might be there for 10. The staff is charged with the entire program when all the weekend warriors have gone back to their day jobs or retirement leisure.

Aw -- did you catch that little sneer? There is often some degree of territorial emotion when others step into our space. Volunteers and employees should understand that. Volunteers should put themselves in the shoes of ministry staff, understanding their perspective, and staff should consider volunteer perspectives. An employee may feel any one or more of the following concerning volunteer activities:

- Does the pastor (or my boss) think I can't do it, so they brought in volunteers to cover my weakness?

- Has some failure on my part led to this group of weekend warriors?

- I've asked for radios for years – how did a volunteer step in here and in three months convince my boss to get them?

- We are spending precious money and time catering to this volunteer effort that I could use a whole lot more effectively.

- We've been doing it this way for 37 years. Why are they now trying to fix what isn't broken?

Any of these trepidations could be partially legitimate, but more than likely they are problems existing only in the 8-inch space between the ears. There could be similar mental smoke rising on the volunteer's side of the relational dynamics:

- Here I am giving my time and they won't listen to my suggestions.

- I'm not paid to be here, but at least I'm equally unappreciated.

- The staff doesn't like me.

- That's just an old church policy – if they care they will follow my suggestions. If they don't, I'm out of here and taking my tithes support with me.

- I have 37 years of experience with this, why do they not believe me when I say…

There could be pages of possible thoughts from both sides of this subject. The point is that both volunteers and employees should work together towards the common purpose of the respective ministry. The intention is to develop a safety ministry. It's not about job security and it's certainly not about recognition. It's about the particular ministry mission and protecting the people and resources of that ministry.

Some business colleagues and I once did a study of the word "customer" and concepts associated with the title. Of the many concepts we explored, two remain as plumb-lines of my personal philosophy regarding customer relations:

> 1. A customer is any person or group of persons with which we have professional interaction. It is not just someone who pays me or my company money -- it is my boss, my coworkers, my staff, the mailman who lays mail on the front counter every day, the guys in the warehouse and custodians emptying trash at night.

> 2. The customer is not always right -- but they are always the customer.

Good leaders should prepare staff for working with volunteers, volunteers for working with staff, and everyone for working with people of all sorts in the ministry environment. In addition to being committed to the ministry's primary purpose; leaders, staff and volunteers need to understand and practice good customer relations between themselves and others they serve.

Volunteers and staff are co-laborers and co-leaders in the effort. Consider jointly developing a mission statement with them for the MST. The very process of working together through the development of program definition promotes coalition.

RECRUITING

Ministry security plans are often started because someone in the organization or congregation was motivated by an event or personal passion to come to leadership. But as the idea migrates into a program, the process of filling all the slots can start to bog down. Once the original person or group has launched the program and begins to define it, there are some effective means of getting the right people to come forward with intentions to serve.

Finding suitable and willing people to serve is easier than many think. In a small church most people know each other, what they do for a living, and the things they are interested in. If there is a doctor or law enforcement officer in the congregation, everyone knows them. Even if there isn't (which is often the case) it's easier for the person who started the program to look around and see people that may for some reason or another be a good fit. Larger churches have a bigger resource pool, and there are several ways to reach the right people. Following are some ways that have worked for others:

> **CERT as a recruiting event;**
>
> Larger communities have active CERT (Citizens Emergency Response Team) programs. Information is at http://www.citizencorps.gov/cert. Churches can sponsor a CERT event and by so doing discover congregants with an interest in serving.

- Pastoral staff recommendations

- Announcements

- Word of mouth

- Community event (such as CERT)

- Small home groups

If you can only do one thing regarding safety and security, put together a team to intentionally manage it for your ministry. Select the right people, and work with them to form a plan. That plan is best modeled specifically to your organization. This team will make all the difference in the ability to effectively safeguard your organization and the people who frequent there. An incident is not the right time to wonder if you should have a team or if you have selected the right people.

Make certain all portions of that team work together and share the ministry culture safety vision. Don't develop a "security department" that holds everything so close they can't co-labor with the ushers and the facility staff. In fact, you may already have most of the team currently in usher and facility positions. You will most likely need to add to those with more volunteers, but never do so at the expense of leaving the ushers and facilities folks behind.

• • •

THE PARTS

Philip Crouse had repaired a door at the Arvada, Colorado Youth With a Mission facility just days before the gunman attacked. The door had not been latching and locking, so Mr. Crouse simply fixed it. The gunman attacked shortly after midnight on December 9th, 2007 intent on killing many young people. After he killed

> **"Do what you can, with what you have, where you are."**
> ... *Teddy Roosevelt,* speaking to reluctant troops preparing for the battle for San Juan Hill.
>
> **Keep it simple -- but get started.**

two, he fell back out the door in the chaos of those moments. But the door latched and locked and the shooter could not get back in to finish his rampage. Mr. Crouse simply recognized a problem and fixed it. He saved many lives that day, but is remembered primarily as one of the two killed.

Get a free risk and vulnerability analysis from your ministry insurance provider or local law enforcement agency. This will help you understand current vulnerabilities and items which can be corrected (such as the door fixed by Crouse) to make the most of existing parts.

There is a wide array of things that make security work, from simple door locks to complex technical systems. Regardless of an organization's budget, there is typically some level of security in their building. A door is good. A door with a lock is better. An electronic access control lock is great. Having an electronic access control system with historical access data, door position monitoring, time of day control, and additional systems integration is fantastic.

Many ministries would rather not spend money beyond the door itself. But when an avoidable incident occurs, the budget (or tolerance for inconvenience) for security enhancement suddenly becomes a priority.

There is a critical relationship of trust to maintain with the professional trade / vendor community. Vendors and suppliers with strong momentum, a broad installed customer base, and a solid reputation in the community typically provide the biggest bang for the buck. They are in the business to make money. The more experienced, dependable and successful they are, the more their expertise is worth.

There is a tendency in ministries to use "Brother Smith" for whatever reasons. He may be just getting into the security business, but his Great Grandpa was one of the founding members of the church, and Brother Smith and his wife both volunteer as Sunday school teachers. Brother Smith might even be offering to donate the equipment and labor. Is the offer for something that you were going to budget for anyway? If not, consider passing on it.

There is an old saying in the seasoned construction community, "Never roof your own church."

I am not saying that there is never a situation where Brother Smith shouldn't be hired. Brother Smith's offer can be considered, but considered with caution. There are a number of things to be careful of. If you give this project to Brother Smith, who else in the church may feel such an obligation is owed to them for that project or some entirely unrelated project? If problems come up during installation, might those problems cause dissention in the relationship, congregation or leadership? What is the ministry's reputation in the community? Is the ministry known as the cheap guys out there that nobody in the professional community wishes to work with?

It is unwise to pay too much for a product or service, but worse to pay (and get) too little. Security and Life Safety systems are far too important to get cheap with. There are lawsuits existing right now where amateur systems gave an impression of protection inconsistent with actual operations due to unprofessional quality, installation, maintenance, or ability. If you acquire security technologies, be careful and diligent in the selection. A false symbolism of security can be deemed negligence in terms of punitive liability.

The risk / vulnerability analysis is the best launching point for your team to start with. As they begin to work the program, they will identify other parts needed.

A Word on Firearms

The debate over firearms in our country exists even within firearm owner circles. Some feel guns should not be allowed on a church security team at all, some feel it is fine to know they are in the audience and will be used if needed, and some feel only law enforcement trained individuals should carry in a church environment. I disagree with all those extremes.

I favor some team members carrying a firearm. But there are absolute pre-requisites. There is nothing like a gun in the hands of a good person to stop a gun in the hands of a bad person. Guns should be allowed on qualified members if:

1. It is within a legal jurisdiction.

2. The ministry leadership endorses it.

3. There is a carefully planned training and qualifications program. It doesn't have to be an expensive or even cost centered course -- but if team members are armed, they should be practicing together and evaluating the environment together.

4. It has been confirmed with the church insurance underwriter.

5. I urge every church to get an attorney to serve (as a team volunteer if possible) on security plan development. If the church has no attorney, this issue of armed defenders is too important to trust to chance. If you have an incident, you will be forced to have an attorney. That shouldn't be the first time you meet -- present this section to him or her for discussion as you develop your own policies.

Protection is needed in our houses of worship, and there are many cases where a firearm is the only protection capable of stopping an assault. In those cases, more people will die if the assault is not stopped.

The firearms debate may rage if your community discovers you use armed defenders in your ministry. You should be ready to address a news conference if you make that decision.

There is a grey line of distinction between an intentional team and *conceal carry* (CCW) members in the congregation. CCW members that are not part of an intentional team are a reality for any team to be aware of -- they are out there. In some states the conceal carry laws exclude the ability to carry a firearm in a place of worship. In states where it is legal (and realistically even in those where it isn't) the truth of the matter is that there will always be a certain number of congregants in the audience who will be carrying deadly force. To just know that and quietly rely on them to "spring to action if needed" is as reckless as burying our head in the sand denying that they are in our congregation.

I am not opposed to the freedom to carry. I am opposed to signs declaring a gun-free zone. If anyone obeys it, it sure won't be the bad guys with guns. But untrained good guys with guns can become a dangerous reality every team needs to be aware of.

There is a sliding scale of realism to understand with this subject which is directly related to the size of the church. In a church of 20 congregants, those CCW members may be "the team." If so they know each other and should train together. If the church has 20,000 in the worship service with an intentional team that has trained together, there will be some unknown CCW holders eager to get involved if a scenario goes down. The bigger the church, the bigger this concern. Train to the specific environment, with the right people for the culture.

To just know you have armed citizens in a congregation can be just as dangerous as not having anyone ready. A team should know each other and actively train together. Even then, there may be strangers who get involved, and extreme caution is crucial as an incident is managed.

It is best to have a designated team authorized and trained to be armed defenders if your laws allow such. If a violent attack occurs at your organization, those trained individuals should manage the attack until they can effectively transition the incident to responding law enforcement agencies. Large congregations lacking trained and equipped members run the risk of off-duty plain-clothes officers who do not know each other, mixed with untrained defenders, all shooting at bad people, each other, and innocent bystanders with panicking crowds diving to avoid the skirmish. And the reality remains, that even with trained operators some of those people may come into the mix. Talk about how your team might handle that scenario.

In a live fire situation, there is plenty of confusion to go around even among team members who know each other and have trained together. Whether the crowd is 20 or 20,000, there will be some measure of chaos.

I don't even hunt with people whom I know little about – I hunt with people I trust around a firearm. Hunting safety is important, and it is that much more important to have a team that has trained together be responsible when an incident is occurring in a crowded environment. Unfamiliar (to each other) responders with guns joining the mix is more likely to happen the larger the church. As much as is realistic, your congregation should know that there is a designated and specific team of defenders should an incident occur.

In just about every major shooting, the possibility of multiple shooters must quickly be considered. At the shooting at New Life Church in 2007, the report of a second shooter was developing even as the shooter was entering the building. Within seconds of hearing that there may be a second shooter, and while taking a position of readiness for the gun battle, I had a total stranger show up behind me yelling in anger. After quickly checking his hands for a weapon (due to the second shooter alert), I told him he needed to get behind me and out of the building. I simply had to make a judgment call he was not the second shooter quickly based upon his demeanor and apparent lack of a weapon.

I use my experience to emphasize the value of having trained armed defenders who know each other and are working as a team, but being ready for those who throw themselves into the mix. Had New Life not had a functioning team that day, the responses to the gunman would have been left to a loose knit group of responders who could have potentially increased injury as they were dealing with the threat. I had a front row seat to the chaos potential.

I hope your authorized armed defenders will never need to reveal their firearm. It is the very last option, and even if drawn it should be their primary hope that they can hold the aggressor at bay until law enforcement arrives, guide those tactical first responders into effective positions, and quickly turn the situation over to them. However, if the speed of the attack is moving too fast to allow for any of this, there may only be one realistic way to resolve it – and the bigger the caliber the better (another front row seat observation I had on the day of our shooting).

Some things to consider:

- Protection of the offering (theft) is not an appropriate use of deadly force. Make sure any on the team who carry understand use of force is only applied when loss of life of others appears certain.

- Eric Harris and Dylan Klebold (the Columbine School shooters) intentionally used solid jacketed bullets for maximum carnage. They purposely wanted each bullet to continue as far as it could inflicting a far reaching field of injury. One of the trainings your team should do is that of discussing bullet types to use. Maximum stopping power with minimum ricochet and wall penetration (exactly the opposite of the Harris / Klebold model) should be a priority.

- Drill on recognizing elements of the deadly triangle (opportunity, intention, and capacity) as team preparation for using deadly force. In order to be considered as a justifiable evaluation that loss of innocent life is certain, the attacker must clearly exhibit the opportunity, intention and capacity (all at once) to kill victims. Drill on active scenarios of two but not all three elements. Drill baby drill.

- Be certain of your own rules of engagement, preferably detailed in a clearly understood response continuum. If a situation goes down, whoever used a firearm to stop the attack will be whisked away by investigators soon after (if they are still alive). Count on them being grilled on the rules -- they better know them off the top of their head. They won't get time for a refresher course on the way to the station. Include that potential ride and interview as part of your team training. How much is your defender going to hold to the "I can't speak until my attorney is present" model? It is a good model, as long as it is within reason. To clam up and not say anything if there are still active bad guys on the scene would be irresponsible. Be reasonable with sharing known information that could benefit the safety of responding officers or congregants still in harm's way. Aside from that, get that attorney who helps your team in there with you.

- Any business gears up with the proper amounts of staff at busier times. Movie theaters have more staff on hand on Friday and Saturday evening than any other time of the week. Electric utilities have more people in the middle of a hot day, and law enforcement has more officers on duty on Friday and Saturday night than any other time. Agencies typically have fewer officers on duty on Sunday morning than any other time of the week. So if you choose to "just let law enforcement deal with any threats", your standard wait of eight minutes might be longer if the wolf comes on Sunday morning.

• • •

THE PROCESSES

To indicate an activity is like a three-ring-circus, conjures notions of undisciplined chaos. On more careful consideration, those who conduct or participate in a three-ring-circus are fairly talented folks with well-scripted coordination.

The dynamics of safety and security in a church environment can be like a three-ring-circus. Good processes provide the definition of how multiple personalities, working in dynamic and unpredictable scenarios, function as a team in a well-orchestrated program. There should be no offense taken by the circus analogy. It can be a positive comparison, or it can reinforce the traditional notions when done wrong.

Good processes are currently working in many mega churches. However they can be applicable to the 334,700 American assemblies smaller than the 1,300 mega churches (2,000 + members) in the USA. Much of what works in a large church will work on a smaller scale, so small churches shouldn't need to reinvent the wheel.

We never know at the planning stage what the details of future incidents will be. The immediate objective will be stopping (or at least mitigating) danger. The final goal is return to normalcy. Actions between the two must be as short and effective as possible.

That says easy.

There are many variations of emergency procedures. Procedural readiness varies from having nothing written at all, to thick binders of jargon that few have the time to read and even fewer can recall when adrenalin is rushing and seconds count. I have been the author of, and am now opposed to, bulky binders of emergency procedures. Keep it simple, but develop and document effective procedures.

As with identifying the parts that need to be corrected or obtained, the best team to develop your processes is your people. There are "cut and paste plans" available out there for a minor investment. This book is a why-to, and those resources provide details for how-to. A Google search for "church security plan" will return options for consideration.

To realize efficiency in any particular job, professionals should participate in an association dedicated to that profession. There is no other association quite like the National Organization of Church Safety and Security Management (www.nocssm.org). Chuck Chadwick is the President of this fine organization, with dedication that spans many years. We all owe it to our profession to get involved in an effort to work with each other to improve understanding and effectiveness in this effort. To this end, I encourage participation in NOCSSM. With membership comes an electronically editable security plan.

Whatever resources or self-study a church or ministry may choose to use for program development should serve them well.

To initiate a program that is never needed isn't a bad thing in this case. It is never wrong to increase situational awareness and readiness.

I hope every reader and security conference attendee can tell me, "Thanks for nothing" someday. I hope you never so much as have a child slip and fall in your hallway. And I really hope you never hear gunfire in your sanctuary.

But some of us have, and some of you will.

CHAPTER 5
Shots Fired!

"Life is not about your story that you invite Him into.
Life is about His story that He invites you into."
Dr. Stephen Trammell

Fifteen days after the first proposal for this book was finished, we experienced the shooting at New Life Church. Edits were needed. In fact, these last two chapters were added. The way the aggressor was quickly and effectively stopped by an intentionally developed church security team set a precedent in church security culture. We would have much rather read about the incident happening somewhere else. But since we walked through it, I will share the experience.

As with any major incident, the story looks and tells differently from various observers' views. I will tell how it went down from my perspective, and then report discoveries of the investigation and interviews that followed. It is not *my* story. It is the story of a team security effort, hosts of witnesses, remarkable church leadership and a significant number of law enforcement, fire and medical first responders. Tragically, it is a story with many victims.

I just happened to be one of many who were directly involved. I will deliver the security perspective, leaving the spiritual and redemption messages to others more qualified in that mission.

● ● ●

I began early every Sunday morning doing intelligence research. December 9th, 2007 began no differently. I found nothing to indicate any threats specific to New Life Church. I put my laptop aside, poured coffee for my wife and we turned on the TV to catch the news.

The news was carrying the story of a gunman who had attacked a Youth With a Mission (YWAM) facility in Arvada 77 miles north of New Life Church. The News gave a description of the unknown gunman and indicated he was still at large. The YWAM folks had no idea why he had attacked them. He had come asking for a room to spend the night. When they had no such room, he produced a gun and started shooting, killing two young people in the senseless rampage.

I racked the leg rest down on my easy chair and reached for the phone. My wife was slightly startled at my instant reaction. I told her I was calling our security team (we call it our "Life Safety Ministry") leader for the day (Jeff Kowell) to tip him off to be ready. She later admitted she thought I was getting paranoid.

I told Jeff about the YWAM attack and why I was concerned for New Life. I was considering the anger might be specific to YWAM, and that the gunman might know a YWAM executive had an office at New Life. Jeff agreed with my concern, and thus began a posture of increased vigilance at New Life Church.

One of our other team members (Tim Priebe) printed a description of the gunman from the internet and brought it with him, as he too had seen the news and was concerned for the same reasons. Lance Coles (church administrator) and I met and as a result called some of the YWAM leaders he knew to determine: A) where the New Life-based executive was and B) what (if any) additional information they might have regarding the shooter. Still reeling from their attack, they didn't have much to offer on the description of the shooter, but did confirm that the executive we were concerned about was not in Colorado that day.

What little information they did have, we added to the paper Tim had printed and made sufficient copies to give to the front desk and others. Of course if we hadn't known the YWAM executive wasn't there, the gunman certainly wouldn't know, so we maintained our vigilance. As we prepared for the first service that morning, Jeff alerted the Life

Safety Ministry volunteer team, extra duty police officers, and ushers of the threat. When I handed one of the copies to a lady working at the guest services desk, she seemed puzzled and asked, "But what does this have to do with us?" I told her we hoped nothing, but we just wanted to be a bit extra vigilant and watch for anyone fitting that description or suspicious behavior. She responded with a dismissive, *OK*, and dropped the paper on the desk in such a way I was certain it would not be looked at again.

New Life is a big place. The property consists of three buildings and more than 2,000 parking spaces on over 30 acres. Our buildings do not lay straight with the compass. As with many buildings in our region, ours were built with a directional orientation designed so prominent rooms and offices have Pikes Peak framed in their most predominant exterior views. So those of us with need of directional reference are familiar with the term "plan-north" (often quite different than "true-north") to describe the orientation of a building.

In the case of the New Life buildings, they are almost 45° northeast of Pikes Peak, and rotated from true north accordingly. So our plan-north is really almost true northwest. Directional references used in this chapter use the plan language (not *true* north, east, south or west).

> The description distributed by news sources that morning was, "a 20-year-old white male, wearing a dark jacket and skull cap. He may have glasses or a beard" (Rocky Mountain News, 12/09/07). This wasn't much to go on in the first place, and there was no beard. Always be careful with first-release descriptions -- they are seldom 100% accurate.

Now that I have thoroughly confused those of you who really don't care about direction, I will attempt to set the scene.

Our main building is in the center of the campus with parking and two other buildings around it. With an 8,000 seat sanctuary on the west end, it comprises nearly 200,000 square feet. Just across a driveway northwest of the main building is a 44,000 square foot special function facility we call The World Prayer Center. Just across a narrow driveway east of the main building is another 15,000 square foot facility we call the Tent (due to the commercial canvas construction -- similar to the roof of Denver International Airport).

That day we had one extra-duty Colorado Springs Police Department (CSPD) officer (Wyatt) roaming the interiors of all three buildings plus two (Chacon and Roman) for the exterior parking and drive areas, consistent with most other Sundays. Mike Steczo (former Chicago PD) served as a New Life associate pastor, chaplain for El Paso County Sheriff's Office (EPSO) and as an armed Life Safety Ministry (LSM) team member. Mike parked his marked EPSO chaplain's car in front of the World Prayer Center (which was where the YWAM office was at that time) as a show of force. Officer Wyatt parked his marked unit in a similar fashion at the north (primary) entrance of our main facility.

● ● ●

Unknown to us at the time, a young man had posted ominous blogs of death between 3:34 and 4:07 that morning. He then went home to sleep, and around 9:30 got up and started blogging again. It was the first of those 10 final diatribes which concluded, "Christian America – this is your Columbine." The others were just as dark. His comments were laughed off or scanned over by most who read them. There was nothing specific about YWAM or New Life Church.

Those web-site comments clearly revealed a young man being taken into ugly clutches of irreversible evil. As some of his fellow bloggers began to read through the multiple postings that morning, they eventually did call 911 on suspicion of a connection to the YWAM murders[22]. But the call came too late. The writer logged off his computer and went mobile again at 11:01 AM[23] and no one knew where he was headed. Though the FBI and Arvada Police Department soon assigned a name to the young man they were looking for, there was no immediate way to make a connection to the killer's additional targets, or even determine with certainty there were more targets[24].

> "I'm coming for EVERYONE soon, and I WILL be armed to the @#%$ teeth, and I WILL shoot to kill and I WILL @#%$ KILL EVERYTHING!"
>
> ...portion of a long message by the shooter under the name of "DyingChild_65" on the blog-site, alt.suicide.holiday at 10:03 AM on the day of the shootings

He was traveling south, with the intention of unleashing the horror accumulated inside of him on as many defenseless people as he could.

He was headed for our church.

• • •

Dr. Jack Hayford -- President of the Four Square Church and King's Seminary -- was our special guest speaker that day. After the service was over, our 19-year-old daughter met with Dr. Hayford and spoke with him from about 12:35 until 12:45.

While they were talking, the LSM volunteer serving executive protection asked me if I could take over for him as he had to leave, which would leave me as the only armed team member aside from the

CSPD officers remaining (or so we both thought). My wife and daughter cordially accepted the inconvenience of waiting around as I would need to stay with Dr. Hayford and Brady Boyd (our senior pastor) until Dr. Hayford would leave for the airport around 2:00 PM. Dr. Hayford and Brady went into Brady's office with a handful of others for lunch as I stood guard outside the door. About 1:00 PM, CSPD officers Chacon, Roman and Wyatt left consistent with the extra-duty agreement. Four other security team members were still on site, although I was only aware of two (Buck Snodgrass and Dave Hagen).

Less than five minutes after the three CSPD officers left, Buck radioed he was investigating smoke at the north building entry (our church's primary vehicle drop-off point where Joe Wyatt's marked unit had been sitting all morning). Buck reported the smoke was from a commercial smoke bomb, and would give updates when he had more information.

> Any time something unusual happens, all security persons should not report to what may appear to be the primary scene. Whatever is happening could be a diversion – these are critical times to have people alert at other vulnerable areas.

Dr. Hayford was planning to say a few words to a group of King's Seminary students gathering in a room off the main hallway, and directly below us before he left for the airport. As time went by with no follow up communication regarding the smoke, I told Brady's secretary I would take Jack and Brady down a back stair when they were ready to go to that meeting because we had something going on in the main entrance area that was unclear.

As I was speaking, I heard shots. I instantly took off towards the shots, still believing I was the only armed defender left on duty. As I ran down the stairs the shots were so loud I had no idea where in the building they were coming from.

As I came to the bottom of the stairs, I saw Buck squatted low in the far west end of the long hallway. He was facing east with both hands out to his sides yelling at people to, "Get back!" That hallway is over 300 feet long and 25 feet wide with smaller hallways off to the sides. It is really more of a long lobby -- in fact it was our previous church lobby before we added the new 8,000 seat sanctuary. As I came into Buck's view he yelled out to me that the shooter was coming through the doors to my left.

I observed the shooter coming in through the exterior doors towards us as I ran towards him. Though he was over 100 yards away, it was clear he was armed with an assault rifle and wearing black tactical clothing. I couldn't see anyone in the hallway at that moment except the gunman, Buck and I. The first thing the shooter would have seen as he entered the building through the doors he had just shot through, was me running at him with a weapon drawn and

> It is possible there were others in the hallway in those opening moments, but adrenalin sets tunnel vision on the primary concern. That reaction works for both the attacker and defender. An attacker's focus (and aim) goes to the armed defender even before shots are exchanged, thus providing one more element of protection for the innocent.

Buck keeping the hall cleared behind me. I later learned of many who had been in that hallway just seconds before the shooter and I started towards each other, and even some who observed glimpses of our positions later.

That would have been when the attacker realized his plans had been changed. He moved to his right, and I moved to my left (thus we positioned building features between us on the north side of the main hallway).

Years before I had bought into the 3-3-5 theory; that most protective gun battles are over in three seconds, rarely are more than three shots fired, and the range is typically less than five feet. With that in mind and for ease of concealment, my carry weapon of choice was a Keltek .32 ACP. It was certainly not the right choice for this situation (and given my experience now, not for many others), but would have to do. I knew his effective range was over 100 yards and mine was 10.

I quickly chose a spot at hallway one for the ensuing gun battle – a position suitable to stop the attacker before he could enter the sanctuary. I chose a point for cover, and planned to ambush the gunman as he came down the hallway past a column I estimated to be 10 yards away from my chosen position. Though I had shot many rounds through that .32, and felt confident at 10 yards, it was overwhelming to realize that little pistol was the only protection between the gunman and the sanctuary, in which many people were still lingering -- including my own wife and daughter.

It became very personal at that moment -- like lightning striking my chest. I knew he had come in shooting, was not there to talk, and one of us would die here. I was confident of getting the first shot when the shooting commenced, and maybe a follow up if needed. Everything in me was determined to make it be over for him before he could return fire.

Looking east -- near arrows shows my route, far arrow indicates shooter's route (tables were not there on the day of the shooting).

As my tunnel vision focused on the column where I expected him to appear any second, I realized my belly was hanging past the corner. With the .32 aimed and steadied on the corner, I leaned down and pulled my belly back just enough so nothing but my pistol and right eye were exposed around that corner as I went into the crouched and ready position.

I started to pray, but was interrupted by a radio transmission through my earpiece that there was a second shooter (other team members later said the transmission was that there *could be* a second shooter – but in my adrenalin-fueled state I simply heard there *was* a second shooter). Instead of praying, I cursed. I could not do anything about the second shooter and decided to leave him to whatever fate someone else may have for him. I couldn't respond on radio as I did not want to make any noise that would compromise my position, didn't feel there was time to use my hands for anything but weapon control, and couldn't release my focus from where I expected to see the attacker any moment.

Seconds after hearing of the second shooter, someone yelled in anger behind me. I turned my head and saw a stranger close to me. I instantly viewed his hands looking for a weapon. Not seeing one, thus feeling confident he wasn't the second shooter, I focused back on the column and told him to get behind me and out of the building. He refused, telling me he was a combat veteran and was going after the shooter. This wasn't the time to argue. Affirmation he wasn't the second shooter came when he asked for my weapon. I made it very clear he would not get my weapon, and repeated for him to get out of there. Instead of leaving, he yelled down the hall at the attacker.

I repeated my demand for him to get out of the building. I yelled it that time knowing he had blown my cover. Another church employee was also coming up the side hall behind me and thought I was yelling at him (I didn't even know he was there). That employee obediently turned and exited the building, but the overzealous friendly would not obey. I would later discover his name was Larry.

Larry said, "Fine then -- I'll go after him without a weapon." He took two steps out to my right, and rapid fire shots rang out as drywall exploded all around us, ricocheting one projectile through the corner above me (right where my head had been just prior to lowering it due to my belly). Debris filled the air, and it felt like hot sand blasting my face. I saw Larry's arm cartwheel, and he jumped back behind me saying, "The (S.O.B.) shot me."

Imagine that.

I took Larry's arm into my hands, quickly determined the wound was superficial, *sighed* a quick prayer for my aim, and resumed my ambush stance and focus. Though I knew my position of cover had been irreparably compromised, it was too late to choose another spot. Now, in addition to an active shooter coming down the hall, I had a complete stranger on my hands telling me how to do my job. This was not the time, yet he was beyond any hope of control. My attention had to be 100% on the column where I was certain the gunman would soon appear.

There was no option but to simply tune the friendly out as much as possible. Then I saw something else I had not seen before.

With tunnel vision focused on the attack, I had missed a frightened boy huddled under a counter between that column and me. Feeling the gun battle was about to commence I could see he would be right in the middle. I stepped out to cover him, and motioned for him to quickly come towards safety to my left. As he passed me I instructed him to get out of the building to my left as I kept my eyes and weapon trained on the column.

Just as the boy cleared, I saw Jeanne Assam (whom I thought had gone home) further down the hallway towards the gunman and on the other side (the gunman and I were both on the north side of the east / west hallway, Jeanne emerged on the south side). I heard her yell something with authority and knew I was about to see her kill or be killed.

Jeanne had been in law enforcement some years earlier, and had joined our team as a volunteer less than a month before that day.

She quickly fired multiple times with her 9 mm.

After firing, she stepped out from her cover and started across with her weapon still drawn. Not being able to see the shooter, I had no idea if he had been hit or escaped. I ran up to get beside Jeanne, and she and I walked cautiously up to where he was laying. He had gone down with his back to the wall, and his feet out in the aisle of hall number four where it joined the main hallway. We kept our weapons drawn and watched as blood pumped from the right side of his head. We watched as his skin color went from pink to white, and the blood flow slowed to a trickle.

He was lying with his head up against the wall, the bushmaster assault rifle lying along his left leg and a Springfield XD 9 mm by his right hand. The rifle was laying in such a way that his finger was still close to the trigger, so I watched his finger for any movement prepared to finish it, but it was increasingly obvious no finish would be needed.

As Jeanne and I stood over the shooter's body with our weapons drawn, she was on the radio and I was trying to get through to 911 on my cell phone. As we were both in that position (Jeanne at his feet and I at his head) Larry came running from behind, slipped between us and jumped over the shooter's body yelling in excitement. As soon as he landed on the other side of the body, he reached down and grabbed the pistol by the shooter's right hand.

As he was raising it into the air, Jeanne and I were both yelling at this stranger to drop the weapon. I later learned Buck had made it back in then as well, and was also yelling at Larry to drop the weapon (with all the adrenalin, I had no idea Buck was there). Larry simultaneously racked the magazine to clear a stove-piped round, and dropped out the clip. then quickly dropped the weapon.

Larry may never know how close he came to dying at that instant. Had he even accidently pointed it in our direction, all three of us would have fired.

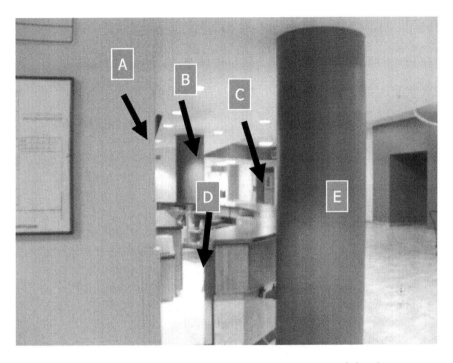

A: Corner I was using as cover. B: Column where I expected the shooter to appear. C: Where Jeanne Assam appeared. D: Where young male was hiding. E: Column that was hit when Larry stepped out from behind me.

Dave Hagen came running back in. He and Buck had both run to their vehicles to retrieve weapons. Dave had been reaching for his Glock .40 in his vehicle when he heard Jeanne announce the shooter was down, and had grabbed his medical bag instead of his weapon, so only Buck returned with a weapon. I yelled at them to get Larry away from the scene. I watched as Larry and Buck got into an argument. Buck was trying to figure out who Larry was and what to do with him. Larry was acting like he was in charge, questioning Buck's credentials. Buck confirmed his credentials by putting his .45 to Larry's head. During that heated exchange I was focused on a pyrotechnic device between Buck's legs on the floor, trying to determine if it was ignited or dangerous. As they argued I decided it must be a smoke bomb, and saw a non-electric ignition which did not appear to be ignited (the observation was correct). So I let them argue as I continued trying to

107

call 911 (I never got through). It was a relief to have someone else deal with Larry for a while.

> Security team members should store direct dial numbers to local law enforcement precincts in their cell phones. If an incident goes down, you may have the best information for law enforcement when you have done your part, but in a crowded environment like a church setting, the 911 system will be overwhelmed.

I also thought Mike Steczo (who I knew carried a .45) had left for the day, but he was in the World Prayer Center when he heard the radio alerts concerning a shooter (probably the one about the possibility of a second shooter), and had taken off as hard as he could go for the main building nearby. Mike realized later he hadn't even taken time to tell his wife (who was standing right next to him) goodbye, he just instinctively ran towards the shooter. It was over by the time Mike got there but he too had run instantly towards the threat.

• • •

Though I would soon learn he had just turned 24 years old, the shooter seemed to be just a boy. I looked over the black tactical clothing and substantial tactical gear (clips, tactical belt, pouches, etc.) he was wearing. In a strange way he appeared very peaceful, though I had extreme and quickly intensifying anger at him. I can't explain the peaceful look – it's just how he was.

Why would he do this?

I found myself alone with him for some time where he had been stopped at hallway four -- just 60 feet inside the door he had come through just moments before.

As intense as my anger was, I can't imagine the rage had I known then of the carnage left in his wake. The fury would build in the next few days to a point of feeling and expressing things I regret. But as I stood beside his lifeless body, my mind was in overdrive replaying all that had transpired in those incomprehensible moments. I hadn't felt stupid as I had in the Kerry Dore incident in 1996 -- my actions this time were more strategic, though it had been instantly obvious the stakes were much higher.

We had been plunged through rapid and extraordinary events. I had been catapulted through a fast action sequence of hearing shots, seeing the shooter, choosing a position, second shooter, Larry, Jeanne appearing, then watching death take over life – all in the hallway of our church. And now I stood in silence looking at a peaceful body. I felt he had no right to be peaceful.

It was just too much to process, and I didn't even know the whole story yet.

I stayed there beside him until law enforcement arrived. When the 4-man tactical team came in through the same doors the shooter had just come through, I slid my weapon out into the hallway and stepped out with one arm high over my head, and the other extended towards the shooter, asserting loud and clear that "the shooter is right here!" without making eye contact with them and keeping my body very still and visible. I stayed in that frozen position as they circled around me and began to look over the body, weapons, ammunition, and incendiary devices around him.

Due to the unknown nature, quantity and positions of the incendiary devices, it was quickly decided to let bomb technicians do further checking (beyond the initial vital signs check the first entry team did). This was about 1:20 PM; it would be 11:00 that night when Coroner Rob Stevenson was able to remove his body[25]. A lot happened in that time span.

After the officers were with the shooter, Mike and I ran up to tell Brady and Jack that a shooter was down, there may be another one, and to remain behind locked doors until further notice. Then we returned down to the shooting scene and began to relay as much as we could to the rising surge of law enforcement.

Law enforcement officers from all agencies were arriving on campus. I watched a congregant show up at the final crime scene with a pistol sticking out of his belt. An EPSO officer beside me yelled at him to put his hands in the air. One of our team eased the tension by telling us he knew him, and that he was OK.

Then we began hearing intense yelling, "Get on the ground! Hands in the air! Put the WEAPON DOWN – GET ON THE (expletives) GROUND!" A hospitality worker was standing a short distance down the main hall from us as I was talking with the EPSO officer. Our conversation was interrupted by the yelling, and we could see this church employee on his cell phone looking puzzled at us, as well as to his left down a side hall we couldn't see down, where the yelling was coming from. The employee slowly started going to the floor, placing his cell phone on the floor with his arms spread wide. It was a responding police officer coming through a side door thinking this man could be a shooter. The EPSO officer and I slowly showed ourselves around the corner to the excited police officer assuring him, "he's OK – he works here -- it's a cell phone."

The intensity of the atmosphere was super-charged and escalating exponentially as officers from multiple agencies converged from all directions responding to the city-wide emergency full call-out. Some congregants were wandering around in shock, others were emerging from hiding, and nobody knew if there was another shooter among us. It became clear that anyone who wasn't law enforcement (including LSM members) needed to be away from all crime scene areas. All of us who were directly involved were taken to the Tent where a command center was forming.

● ● ●

As soon as I got into the Tent facility, Dave pointed out a lady sitting at a table with two young girls. Dave told me she had just seen her husband shot, and he asked me to go speak with her.

I had heard just before we were moved away from the final crime scene that two women had been shot in the parking lot and were being attended to by medical professionals. I had quickly gotten through to my wife and daughter by cell phone, but upon confirming their safety it was almost as if I couldn't take more information in just yet -- I wasn't ready to accept it. And now I was hearing that perhaps a man had been shot as well. I was having trouble putting it all together.

I knelt down beside her and could see her hands were covered in blood. As she began to tell me her story, I could not help but break a first-aid rule, I took her blood-soaked right hand in mine.

The two women I had heard of were her daughters, one just 18 years old and the other only 16. Her husband had been shot as well. She did not know (or more likely just could not bring herself to say) the conditions of her daughters, or that of her husband.

How could so much hostility be unleashed on one family?

I tore a piece of paper off a nearby tablet, and asked her for her name and the names of her family. I wrote as she told me their last name was Works. Her name was Marie, and I wrote the names of her daughters as she told me – Gracie, Laurie, Stephanie and Rachel. She said her husband was David. She told me the two girls shot were Stephanie and Rachel. She asked me to pray for her other two daughters there with her.

As I prayed for all of them, I felt like the most unqualified person on the planet. My heart ached as I pictured the attacker's weapon I had just encountered, and considered the shooting experience she was describing to me. I knew it couldn't be good, prayed hard, but my prayer felt hollow, weak, and incompetent. As I began to pray, I noticed one of our LSM medical team members (Dr. Olivier) across the table with an exhausted, empty look in his eyes.

When I concluded that shallow feeling prayer, I told her I was going to find a pastor to be with her. Dr. Olivier got up and joined me as I walked away. As we moved out of hearing distance from Marie, he told of how he had been the first medical professional to them, and had stayed with them in the parking lot until EMTs began to arrive and take over. He was certain of the imminent fatality of Rachel, believed Stephanie was already gone, and that David was in very serious condition with life threatening wounds. He said paramedics were preparing to transport them when he had escorted Marie, Gracie and Laurie into the tent.

I described the situation to some CSPD officers who appeared to be taking charge, told them where Brady was in the main building, and asked if we could get Brady down to be with Marie. The officers were emphatic and rigid in their determination to not let anyone move until second shooter and potential explosives issues were resolved.

I am not implying dissatisfaction with their rigidity, as they were just doing their jobs. There are few easy or feel-good options in a developing significant incident like that. As various agencies and authority levels are coming in, command decisions and communications are a developing process at best. There was some understandable confusion that is simply part of the story, but disorder is not the anchor memory associated with law enforcement actions that day.

Many of us (Marie, Laurie and Grace Works, the security team, and other direct witnesses) were a growing crowd in the tent. Pastor Brady and Jack Hayford were still in the main building, and a group of other pastors were restricted to the World Prayer Center. The interim officers in charge made it very clear to me that they understood the gravity of the situation, but extreme caution was the current mandate, nobody was moving, and this was no time to talk about victim feelings.

The misery of those moments was overwhelming. Innocent lives had been taken, and I had been too late to participate in the negotiation. I couldn't change it or make anyone feel better about it.

I knew if it were my wife, she would want nothing more than to be with her family. I turned my attention from law enforcement to arriving paramedics in an effort to get Marie and her daughters transported. I was finally able to get a paramedic crew to understand the situation, and they at least went over to talk with Marie. I could only hope they were getting serious about plans to transport her and her girls to be with their injured family members.

I saw Jeanne standing at a small bistro table by the north window of the Tent entry area with a water bottle. Mike Steczo was with her. I confirmed she was doing OK. She seemed incredibly calm, and Mike assured me he would not leave her side. She asked me where she had hit him, and where all that blood was coming from. I told her it looked to me like it was coming from the right side of his neck, and that she must have hit a carotid artery (we would later discover I was wrong in that assertion) due to the way the blood was pumping so far. I reassured her she had done the right thing then turned my attention again towards Marie Works.

Before I made it to Marie's table, I was surprised to see Brady, Dr. Hayford and a team of pastors walking into the tent. It was obvious some officers were making different decisions, the ones I had spoken to had changed their mind, or Brady and crew had simply come out on their own and walked over to the tent. Regardless, I was relieved to see them walking in. As I made it to Brady, he was raising his hands and inviting everyone to gather around for prayer. As people gathered I quietly informed him what I knew about the Works family and pointed his attention towards Marie who seemed to be in another world, even though she was just a few feet away.

It seemed as if the air escaped him in anguish as he absorbed the information. I led him to the table where Marie was still seated with Laurie and Gracie. Relieved he was there, I slipped back into the growing crowd as he and Dr. Hayford took over ministry to her.

As soon as they were done praying for her, the church's attorney motioned for Brady, Jack and I to follow him to an area behind some curtains. He asked me to give a quick rundown of what had gone down in the hallway. It was the first I had told anyone of the details.

When I came back into the Tent entry area, Jeanne was standing with officers and pointed towards me. They motioned me over. Homicide detective Mike Happ gave me his business card and instructed me not to talk to anyone except him about what I had seen. He told me they were taking Jeanne to the Police Operations Center to interview her, and when that was done he would call me to come down. He took my cell phone information and they left.

A paramedic assured me plans were being made with CSPD to take Marie and her daughters to the hospital. Around 3:00, CSPD officer Peter Quick transported them to Penrose Main Hospital.

As soon as Mike Happ and Jeanne Assam left, I was asked to report to the CSPD mobile tactical command unit to go over church floor plans with the tactical team leader. I knew by then of where some people were hiding in rooms. For example, pastor Mel Waters had called me about his sons who were still in his office, but he was restricted to the World Prayer Center by law enforcement. It would be much later (3:52 PM) when the tactical team entered Mel's office and released his sons who had been hiding under a desk the entire time.[26] There were many similar stories.

As I moved from the Tent to the mobile tactical command unit I walked across the parking lot where crime scene tape was being strung out and numbered placards being placed. I had to carefully watch my step on the ice-covered asphalt as empty shell casings were scattered all over, and I was trying not to kick them around (though it was accidently kicking one that got my attention in the first place). I could see a white van off to my left with all of its doors open and shattered glass. Based on what Marie had told me, I realized this was their van. It looked as though it had come through a war zone.

I saw Officer Wyatt standing on the passenger side of the van and slightly behind it, as if he was standing guard. We didn't speak, but just merely nodded our heads at each other from a distance as I passed by. Neither of us had any words for what we were in the midst of at that moment. It was bitter cold, and one of my burning memories of that day is seeing Joe stand there almost at attention throughout the long afternoon. I will never forget that look of despair written in stone on his face. Joe is as fine a police officer as you would ever find, and he knew the attack had started as he drove away that afternoon. By the time he turned around and got back to the church, it was over. He too was robbed of any opportunity to participate in the negotiation for lives of the innocent.

• • •

The tactical response had transitioned to a systematic room by room search for a second shooter and / or secondary explosive devices and / or unknown hostages. As with many major crime scenes, law enforcement had to make certain there were no such dangers still active. I was introduced to the officers I would be working with in the command unit, and we began to go over church floor plans in that large RV equipped as a sophisticated tactical support center.

Many monitors were on the wall of the vehicle, and camera operators were scanning the ground along the outside walls of the church, methodically looking for anything out of place. Radio transmissions informed us of the inside tactical team locations and discoveries, and I would show the command center team on a map just where the reports seemed to be coming from, and where I knew of people to be hiding. The interior team came to a door that required a pass-code, so I gave the command center my pass-code and they entered the accounting office, but then set off motion activated intrusion alarms. They quickly checked for inhabitants or threats and moved on shutting the door behind them to isolate the sound as best they could, as I made calls to find someone in accounting who knew the code to silence it.

Once it seemed they had a fairly systematic way of going through the buildings, there was less communication required between the tac team and me. The mobile unit commander told me to make myself comfortable, and they would ask me questions as needed. They brought me water. I hadn't realized how dry my throat was.

I sat at a small table listening to radio chatter that seemed to fade off into the distance. I watched the monitor images as various cameras searched around the buildings for explosives. One monitor was even carrying the Bronco's / Chiefs game, but was being interrupted by news reports of our crime scene. I could tell the news media was showing up, and the first person I saw interviewed was Larry. I could see the tactical command unit we were sitting in on the news.

It seems as though I sat at that little table in the mobile command unit longer than I was at any other location that day. At some point I noticed I had messages on my cell phone. I had never heard it go off. Among the messages was one from Lance Coles recorded at 1:15 in the afternoon. His voice was very calm as he described to me that he had just seen a gunman firing rounds, and had watched the gunman enter the east end of the building. Lance went on to tell me in his calm voice that his son was somewhere in the building. Another message was from my wife telling me they had been released to go home by law enforcement, but that I had the car keys. Once I had learned of their safety, I had become so overcome by aftermath activities it had never occurred to me they would need the keys to go home (or even that I had keys). A CSPD chaplain friend of our family found me about then and took the keys to her.

I decided it would be a good time to write down my account of what had transpired. I pulled out the piece of paper with the Works family notes, and thought at first it wouldn't be near enough paper. But try as I might, I could not bring myself to write more than a few loosely associated words. My pen hand was as dry as my throat. It would be much later before I could bring myself to document things.

Eventually an officer came and told me there was a new "unified command center" (UCC) being set up in a building at the Pikes Peak Community College across the parking lot from New Life Church. I was asked to go there and represent New Life where all involved agencies would be converging in the UCC as the Tent was transforming into a witness interview area.

So I stepped out of the mobile unit and started for the UCC. Another officer stopped me and said the tactical commander needed to see me back in the mobile unit. I went back to the mobile unit. He wasn't there and none of the officers there knew why I had been told to come back. They said the commander was busy in the interview area. So I started back for the UCC.

I made it across the parking lot to the UCC and became active with a group of officers raiding rooms for white boards and easels that we carried to a classroom being set up for the UCC. I reported to the UCC commander, but before I could sit down was informed over radio that a homicide investigator wanted to see me.

It was 5:00 PM when I walked back into the Tent interview area expecting to see Mike Happ. Instead I was introduced to homicide detective Rob Meredith. I kindly told detective Meredith I could not give him my statement as I had promised Mike Happ I would not speak to anyone else. Another officer overheard me say that, and

117

introduced himself as being the supervisor of both Happ and Meredith and assured me he would relay to Mike that he had given me permission to speak with Meredith. So Rob found a table for us. He had no way of knowing the table he chose was the one Marie Works had been setting at when I first met her around 1:30 that day.

Rob sat down in the chair Marie had been in, and I sat next to him where Dr. Olivier had been during that stressful prayer time. It helped to let out some of the story, but I found it hard to recall details. It was as if my brain was drained. I'm not certain of the most effective time for an interview to take place after traumatic events, but I think 3 ½ hours afterwards might not be the best time, but it was better than two hours after when I had first tried to write it down.

But detective Meredith was a professional. He wanted to know what Jeanne said before she fired on the attacker, and I simply could not answer that. I told him all I could say is that it was quite authoritative, but very brief. He wanted to know if there were any follow up shots after she fired her first volley. I told him there were not. He then turned to questions related to the shooter, trying to determine if he had acted alone.

As we were sitting there in the interview, the tactical team was still carefully searching through the large building attempting to secure it. Rob's questions were quite focused on the possibility of accomplices. He wanted to know who had called me on radio concerning the second shooter. I simply had no idea. In my mentally exhausted condition I even told him it could have been Gene Ferrin (which I knew as soon as I said it that it couldn't have been. Gene was the one who had turned over Pastoral protection to me around 12:45 that day because he had to leave).

I recall feeling the same inadequacy I had felt at that very table earlier that day. Why hadn't I looked over the shooter better? I couldn't even recall if he had glasses. It seemed he had gloves on, but at the same time I knew that I had kept a close eye on his trigger finger for movement and it was a bare finger. I would later learn the shooter had a black glove on his right hand and none on his left.

Then as Rob was searching for clues about a second shooter, came the question that clearly evidenced how poor of a crime scene investigator I had been. Rob asked me if the shooter was wearing a microphone or radio technology of any kind. I was stunned. What a perfect thing to have looked for as we were trying to determine if there was a second shooter. But I honestly had no idea. I hadn't thought to look for that in spite of the fact it made perfect sense. Rob was very gracious with me, as he could probably tell how upset I was at myself for not even thinking to look for that. He told me I had processed a lot of information in a short amount of time, and not to get hung up on what I didn't know – just continue telling what I could as best as I could.

All I could tell him was that I never saw any evidence of a second shooter, nor did I believe there ever was a second shooter.

I could see a group of my fellow LSM team gathering around a table nearby. Buck was there, but all the others were LSM members who had returned to the church upon hearing the news. When Rob finished his interview I went to the table of my team mates and sat down with them. It was good to be back among friends, and I must have been at the end of my capacity to deal with command center stuff anymore, as I simply forgot to go back to the UCC. It never occurred to me until the next day I had forgotten all about the UCC when the interview with detective Meredith ended.

As I sat down, I saw Rob Caudle across the table from me. If any one man should be credited with starting the Life Safety Ministry of New Life Church it would be Rob. I had met Rob in the spring of 2005 when he, Roger Harrington and Mike Steczo welcomed me into the developing safety / security team under the supervision of Lance Coles. Rob would be the last person to desire credit, but it is due to him and those other early pioneers that we had been ready that day. It was Rob more than anyone else who not only saw to it that the safety ball started rolling, but has stayed active with the program as an LSM volunteer for the many years since.

As much as Rob Caudle was responsible for raising the issue of safety planning at New Life, our church administrator was to be credited with hearing the call for action clearly. Had Lance Coles not been willing to champion the unpopular concepts of safety and security, the program would have never gotten off the ground.

And to make sure a portion of the program focused just on security, Roger Harrington, with his law enforcement background, and the support of Mike Steczo, was the man who developed the security team. It was Roger who first introduced that controversial idea of having armed security volunteers in the church. Though Roger was no longer on our team, I called him that night to thank him for his early vision and past leadership.

Kim Welsh was one of our LSM team members who had come to the church upon hearing the news. Kim and his wife Kim (seriously -- you can't make that kind of thing up. We call them "Kimhe and Kimshe") are friends of ours, and were both there at the table. After a few minutes sitting with them, I just wanted to go home. I had not seen my wife or daughter since before the shooting, and the sun had set as Kim and Kim drove me home.

It was good to be home and hold my wife as we cried and prayed for the Works family. As I told her a few things about the shooting I began to recall details I had left out with Rob Meredith. I knew I would need to call him to fill in some gaps, but that could wait. My wife told me how our daughter had just come across the parking lot from the Tent to the main building sanctuary just seconds before the shooting started. I told them how the shooting had been quite intense right where she crossed, and where she had come down that long hallway.

My wife had immediately grasped what was happening as she heard shots and saw people run into the sanctuary yelling. She had pulled our daughter to the floor and huddled over her to protect her. The sounds were horrifying. Being very familiar with guns and shooting, she really thought it was a fully automatic rifle (probably due to the echo effects). Our daughter felt bad that her mother was covering her. It helped to reach up and put her arms over her mother's head.

Then my wife had wanted out of there. They stood up and ran out the doors and across the driveway to the World Prayer Center (WPC). At first someone held them up at the door and said something was wrong and nobody was allowed in the building. Her immediate instinct was to start looking for bushes to hide our daughter in. But as more people began promptly pouring out of the main building towards the WPC, they did open the doors and many found refuge in that facility. We never discovered who had ordered the doors locked at first.

My wife and daughter had been moved around with a lot of people as law enforcement tried to process through the possibilities of the second shooter or accomplices. As the shooting had erupted, most people fled to their vehicles and left the campus. About 200 however ended up in the WPC, and they were under the direct and continuing command of law enforcement for several hours. It was 2:40 that afternoon before any were even allowed to use the restrooms.

Among the many things my wife and others in the WPC did not know, was that earlier that afternoon, CSPD had received reports that a "suspicious skinny white male" was seen entering the WPC with a metal device over his left shoulder. Another report indicated someone was on the roof of that facility. Both male and female undercover plain clothes detectives had gone in to intermingle with the crowd for some time to try and locate anything or anyone that seemed suspicious[27].

Around 3:30 that afternoon, the decision was made to start letting congregants go. An interview line was set up in the WPC, and critical contact and identification information was recorded from 183 people as indirect witnesses. Some of those recorded were only listed as representing their family (my wife was recorded, but not our 19-year-old daughter who was with her). Anyone in the WPC interviews that indicated they had been a direct witness, were escorted to the Tent for more intensive interviews. Detail statements were taken that day from over 125 direct witnesses and victims in the Tent building[28]. It was a massive police interview process, and people were relieved to finally be allowed to go home as they were cleared one by one and escorted to their vehicles by law enforcement.

As the day progressed, everyone's attention became more focused on the lives that were still hanging in the balance. I had found out that Dr. Olivier was correct. Stephanie was gone. She had not even been removed from the van where she had been pronounced deceased.[29] We knew that Rachel and David were in critical condition, and that Rachel was barely clinging to life.

About 10:15 that night, Rachel died.[30]

I couldn't rest at home, so about 8:15 PM returned to the church. It was still a sea of police vehicles with flashing blue and red lights reflecting off everything in the cold dark night. I parked out on the street to walk in. I was not allowed to re-enter the scene and was turned away by officer Jason Armas whom I did not know, nor did he know me[31]. Later that night however, I was called and asked to return to the scene and report to the investigative lead -- Sgt. Jeff Jensen -- as the Tent building was cold and they needed the heaters turned on (they had gone off on timers about 10:00 that night). As soon as I got the heat back on, I asked Sgt. Jensen if he needed anything more and he asked me to stay around in case other things came up. I sat alone as the only civilian in a beehive of police activity well into the night.

At around 11:00 PM Sgt. Jensen asked me to work with Officer Wilson to lock doors, turn off ovens in the kitchen, secure café cash registers and similar tasks as he secured the facility for the night.

I got home for the last time on that long day at 1:00 Monday morning. Sleep was hard to find. All I could think about were the coulda-shoulda-wouldas missed that resulted in innocent deaths.

If only…

CHAPTER 6
Through Clearing Smoke

As the sun rose and smoke cleared, the pieces began coming together regarding the entire chronology of events. Law enforcement detectives from Colorado Springs and Arvada had interviewed hundreds of witnesses and victims, and examined an abundance of evidence to put together the whole story. Some witnesses provided great details, others saw things that were unrelated yet in their own mind had to be, and were determined to tell the story from their perspective. Some were directly involved witnesses (like Dave Hagen) that slipped away quietly without ever being interviewed. Some who weren't there spoke as if they were.

THE SECOND SHOOTER

As near as we can tell, the shooter had strategically waited until Officer Wyatt left in his marked police vehicle before igniting the first smoke bomb at our north entry. Some moments later he ignited one at the south entry, but that one was stomped out in disgust by a congregant passing by.[32] Buck and Dave were investigating the north entry smoke, when someone told them they had seen the smoke tossed from a red Toyota with up to three people in it. Buck sent them in to Jeanne Assam who took their statement. It was this report that caused so much concern about a second shooter[33]. All any of us can guess is that this couple simply saw something from their perspective that was not accurate. There was never any evidence, or other reliable witness accounts that revealed any more than one shooter.

The impact of the inaccurate report of a second shooter was far reaching. The second shooter rumor spread like wildfire through the church even before law enforcement arrived. In any mass shooting accomplices must be considered. But in a situation where the reports of such are part of the opening communications of the attack, everything anyone saw that could be a clue had to be followed up on.

Anyone hearing shots and the rumor would understandably suspect everything. Some who saw confusing things made assumptions once they heard about a second shooter and put together their own story to make sense of the senseless.

Part of what was complicating the situation was the widespread crime scene. It was already apparent that the shooter or shooters had used diversion tactics (the smoke bombs), but with it still unknown whether there were accomplices, a shooting at a mall across town had to be considered as related. It was only a few days after the Omaha Mall shooting, and with the question of a relationship between New Life and the Mall, all hospitals in the area went into immediate lockdown.

While it was unknown if the Citadel Mall shooting was related, what was known is that witnesses and victims were spread in a wide area, so accomplices could be as well. Some victims had raced away driving themselves to various hospitals. Calls were coming from all across the region from witnesses who had left the church and then called in to tell what they had seen or heard. Investigators were at all hospitals, and on scene, and in parking lots and streets nearby where vehicles had bullet holes. Witness stories varied greatly in their accuracy. One witness reported that an accomplice was beside a Tahoe which he jumped into and left the scene. Considerable effort was invested looking for a Tahoe with a license plate that began with "660" and a passenger side window shot out (all the witness could recall). Other officers at one of the hospitals found the vehicle of victim Judy Purcell (a Sequoia with a license plate starting in "690") sitting in the hospital parking lot with its windows shot out.

Investigators had to hear it all, compare notes and discover truth in the process. The investigative coordination efforts were phenomenal. And it was happening in an adrenalin-induced environment where nobody knew if a coordinated attack was still developing, or if the attack of a single gunman had ended nearly as soon as it had begun.

Some ladies hiding in a bathroom heard someone open the door and yell, "Is anybody in here?" Even though it was someone trying to rescue them and announce that the attack was over, these ladies remained quiet, hidden and horrified thinking it was the shooter or an accomplice trying to lure them out. They had no way of knowing who fired the many shots they had heard, whether the shooter was down, or if all defenders were down (in fact, they probably didn't know there were armed defenders). It was 45 minutes later before the tactical team made it to that bathroom and finally convinced them it was OK to come out (after first showing extreme tactical readiness towards them and demanding that they throw down their purses). They later told of how they huddled in a back corner, realizing they couldn't stand on a toilet to hide their feet from under the stall doors because the toilets had auto-flush mechanisms on them and would activate, giving away their positions. The final part of their trauma was being briskly walked by officers past a place in the long hallway where they were told to not look left, but look forward and to their right as they passed portions of the crime scene. They could only imagine who or how many victims could be laying there so close to them[34].

One group locked themselves in a classroom with a witness who had seen the shooter coming across the lot and thought (because of his tactical look) he was a rogue cop. So everyone hiding in that room was convinced to remain quiet and hidden regardless of who called out to them.

Among other things, detectives were searching for clues of a second shooter. The police reports are full of stories of folks who are probably certain to this day that they saw a suspicious or likely person. One of those suspicious persons was probably me from the description I read in the report where a witness saw Jeanne and a man with a gun near her as she was firing across the hall[35]. There was even a map drawn that showed my position -- I'm glad that witness didn't have a gun. There are many good reasons to have a specific armed team that trains together.

Roy Pollete was an usher. He had been in the briefing that morning and had been told to be on the watch for suspicious persons or actions. About 11:10 that morning he had spotted a man appearing suspicious in a black Audi. It was suspicious enough that he had reported it to security, but also reported that the vehicle had left when he saw Roy looking at him. Roy was 70 years old and retired from the U.S. Army. Around 1:10 that afternoon, his defensive nature engaged again when, as he helped his wife into the driver's seat of their car, they heard gun shots.

As he ordered his wife to get out of there in the car, Roy started on foot the other way towards the gunfire. As the gunman was outside the east doors shooting into a vehicle, Roy looked around the nearby southeast corner of the building and saw what he thought was an accomplice or combatant get into a vehicle and leave[36]. He then saw the shooter shooting into the church. The *accomplice* Roy saw was probably Matt Purcell (his story later), but it would take time to sort through all that.

Delbert Young was an usher as well. He too had been briefed to be extra vigilant that day. At around 1:10 he was walking towards his vehicle in the north parking lot when he heard gunfire. Just as (unknown to him) Roy was working towards the gunfire from the southeast side of the building, Delbert headed towards the gunfire from the northeast side of the building. As he looked around the northeast corner of the building, he too saw the gunman shooting into the building. 22 years in the army had its effect on Usher Young as well, and his concern for innocent people surpassed that of his own safety.

Delbert stepped out to draw the shooter's attention. The shooter stopped and turned his attention to him. As Delbert dashed back behind the cement corner, he heard more shots. Then he looked back around, and saw that the shooter was entering the building. Delbert ran west to intervene and warn as many people of the coming attack as he could[37].

Mr. Young's actions probably saved lives. When you read later of how quickly Buck Snodgrass and Dave Hagen cleared the hallway of children, it is obvious how every second counted. Buck and Dave were given a few seconds of the shooter's focus being elsewhere by Delbert's actions.

Nonetheless Delbert is 6'2" tall, and was wearing a dark trench-coat that day.

So as one congregant was running to his car, carrying his six-year-old daughter as they were hearing continuous gunfire, he saw Delbert at the corner. Because Young did not appear to be scared, it caused the congregant to report it as he saw it. The tall black man in a dark trench coat at the northeast building corner had to be considered as an accomplice -- just because of his calm demeanor, position, trench coat and how he ran towards an entry as others were running out of it.

As that congregant raced away in his vehicle, his little girl told him she saw a man on the roof with a gun. Her descriptions to the investigator at 8:00 that night were detailed -- black hat, white shirt, and a big gun.[38] His 911 call as he raced away was just as descriptive.[39]

The Police helicopter spotted footprints in the snow on the roof of the WPC. A window screen had been removed from an upper level room and someone had climbed out the window and onto the roof. It had to be considered.

There was an abundance of suspicion concerning that potential second shooter, and increasing dialogue between Arvada and Colorado Springs authorities as the possibility of a connection to the YWAM murders was being investigated.

Then at 2:44 that afternoon, a man called into Colorado Springs 911 saying, "I just shot up the church and I'll shoot it up again." Then the caller simply hung up.

The area JTTF (Joint Terrorism Task Force) including CSPD, EPSO, Pueblo Police Department, ATF and FBI all responded. A massive and quick connecting of the dots led first to the man who had bought the phone the call came from, then to a location the call had originated from (which was a friend the phone's owner had loaned it to). After first coming up with many stories (including that his own children may have done it) the father of four finally admitted to doing it as a joke, adding he was embarrassed and sorry[40].

It was after 9:00 PM when the search for secondary devices and / or shooters came to an end. During that time, the search team opened every possible door in the 198,000 square foot main building. If the master key didn't work, they used their *AXE Master* key. Several thousand dollars' worth of doors were busted open in such a way because the church had drifted away from the Knox-box master key in the 17 years of occupying the facility.

There are those out there who remain convinced to this day of a second shooter. Some because of something they saw or heard (or heard about). But there are always some associated with, or excited about a major issue who thrive on conspiracy theories. A website went up very soon promulgating conspiracy theories about our incident. There is no evidence to support it, nor do those of us directly involved have suspicions there was ever a second shooter.

• • •

An entire book could be written on the shooter's actions leading up to the moment of his death in the hallway. But the purpose of this book is security, so the portions of his story that are relevant as lessons learned for other church security teams are carried here, emphasizing the New Life Church portion of his attack. We now know that he had attacked the Arvada YWAM before coming to New Life Church (NLC).

The shooter had turned 24 years old on Wednesday before he went on his killing spree that Sunday. His birthday -- December 5th -- was the day Robbie Hawkins went on his killing spree at the Westroads Mall in Omaha killing eight people before taking his own life.

On the day of the Westroads Mall shooting, the YWAM / NLC shooter wrote in a blog,

> *Sounds like one of the Nobodies became a Somebody...sure he's still hated by everyone, that is obvious, but at least now he's a somebody.....and he's left a world that didn't give a sh** about him to begin with.*[41]

Earlier blog entries went back to at least September of 2006. In a posting on September 4th of 2006, he had written with disgust of being at New Life Church two years earlier. He told of a debate he had gotten into with a couple of New Life employees. He said they watched him after the debate to see who he was with, then after seeing him with his mother seized an opportunity to talk to her.

According to him, they convinced his mother he was "not walking with the Lord and could be planning violence." He angrily told of how his mother brought pastors to their Denver home from another church, looking for bad books, DVDs, an Xbox and related games and anything else "evil." He wrote of how they destroyed $900 worth of such items. After many disagreements with YWAM, King's Kids and other religious entities, he said that experience caused him to finally turn away from Christianity.[42]

A few months later he took great delight in joining with many other bloggers celebrating Ted Haggard's exposure in immorality[43]. His writings became darker in time as he adulated dark groups, individuals and subjects such as Thelema, Kabalistic and Ceremonial Magick, Marilyn Manson, Hermeticism, the Golden Dawn, Theosophy and others.

He seemed to practically worship Aleister Crowley (Occultist known as the founder of Thelema and other satanic worship) writing often of him. Many of his blogs would contain lyrics of black metal groups such as Slipknot and end with quotes from Crowley.

> Ricky Rodriquez was raised in a cult that is misrepresented by some as being Christian. His childhood was one of awful abuse, which he avenged in 2005 with the brutal murder of Angela Smith in Tucson, Arizona. He killed himself a few days later. He left behind a video, filmed just moments before he killed Smith detailing his plans and reasons. That video is still widely distributed on the internet, and was linked to by the New Life shooter as part of his last day blog posts.

Perhaps no posts would be as telling as those on his last day revealing his high regard for Eric Harris (one of the Columbine shooters) and Ricky Rodriguez. Years of indicators unheeded by his circle of friends and fellow bloggers ended at 11:01 Sunday morning December 9th, 2007 as he logged off for the last time in his life and drove south to New Life.

We don't know how long he may have waited for CSPD to leave, but we do know that after he ignited smoke bombs at the north and south entries, he parked his car in the Tent parking lot with seven empty spaces between his car and the Works' family van sitting at light pole 4, not far from the east entry of our main building. There are three main entries to the main building – the north, south, and east. The east entry is primarily a children's entry, as it opens into that long hallway, with other hallways going off to the sides where classrooms are located.

He sat for some time in his car before he got out. What was he thinking? Was he imagining people horrified by smoke at the north and south entries, resulting in a panicking crowd escaping towards him as he would meet them coming in the east entry? Was he waiting for security to go to the north and south smoke providing him an un-resisted attack in from the east? For reasons we will never know, he waited for the right time.

Jesse Gingrich had just seen her friends -- Rachel, Laurie, and Stephanie Works as they walked past her vehicle towards theirs. Jesse hadn't seen the shooter pull in, but did notice when he got out of his vehicle. She watched as he calmly walked to the back of his Maroon 1992 Toyota Camry and opened the trunk. Knowing New Life has lots of youth activities, skits and such, she thought nothing of it as she watched him pull the black rifle out and put on a backpack. She was thinking the whole time that it was a toy or replica and that there must be

> Make certain your congregation knows there will never be a skit using deadly looking weapons or explosions in your church.

some kind of skit activity going on where young people may be training for overseas missions in countries with terrorists.

Her calm observations were shattered when he aimed the gun at the van sitting just in front of hers and to her left under pole 4. She heard loud shots and saw glass exploding in the windows.[44]

The assault had begun

He walked as he continued shooting into the Works' family van. Marie was in position to drive, and David was in the front passenger side. Laurie had made it into the far back right seat, with Grace beside her to the left. Stephanie was seated right behind her mother, and Rachel was searching through her purse for something just before she would have stepped up into the right side of the center seats.[45]

18-year-old Stephanie was hit and probably died instantly. 16-year-old Rachel was hit hard and went down on the pavement. David was hit twice as he tried to reach Rachel, and went down not far from her.

David had yelled at everyone to get down as soon as the shooting started. Had they not heeded his urgent plea, there would have been more injury in their family. The shooter walked around the front of their van continuing to shoot into it, then turned his attention to his right as he continued towards the main building.

Clayton Meininger and his wife Mary had just dropped off clothes for a donation inside the north entry of the church. They had seen a smoke bomb going off, but had continued with their plans. After they unloaded the clothes they got back into their Ford Explorer and started eastbound along the north side of the main building. At the northeast corner of the building, they turned right and drove south between the Tent building and the east entry doors of the main church building. 11-year-old Clinton was seated behind Clayton, Mary in the front passenger seat, and 14-year-old Haley was behind Mary.

Passing between the buildings, they heard shots. Clayton saw a shooter firing into a white van parked south of the Tent facility. The shooter was estimated to be 30 yards to their left as they watched in disbelief as glass shattered throughout the white van and the shooter deliberately and calmly walked and shot. Mr. Meininger accelerated hard and exited the parking lot.

Nobody in the Meininger vehicle ever saw the shooter turn towards them. This was possibly due to Mary yelling at them to get down, and Clayton focusing on getting out of there. As they were driving away, Clinton reported he had felt something on his leg and that it was hurting. When they were a safe distance away, Clayton pulled over and checked his son over for injuries. Clinton's leg had stung for a little bit, and there was a purple spot about the size of a quarter on the outside of his left leg. He said it first felt like wind on his pant leg.

No bullet or fragments were ever found, and his pain subsided. But investigators discovered where a bullet had fully penetrated through the door. The bullet would have come through right where the discomfort was on Clinton's leg. After shooting one time into the

Meininger vehicle the shooter turned his aim to the vehicle following them[46].

Christina Wilke was southbound between the two buildings as well after completing her duties for the day as a Sunday School teacher. She heard some "pops" and felt her car jolt. She thought something was wrong with her car, or that she had run over something. She looked in her rear view mirror and saw nothing except a man walking across behind her car carrying a rifle. She thought he was a policeman, and wondered for a brief moment why he had his rifle out. Her attention was quickly diverted though as her check engine light came on and she smelled something.

She stopped and got out to look at the front of her car to see what had caused the noise, jolt, engine light, and smell. As she looked at the front left area of her car, she saw two holes. As she was trying to make sense of everything she was hearing, seeing, feeling and smelling she became aware of a white van beside her with the windows shattered. She could see someone crawling beside the shattered van then became aware of the sounds of shooting and screaming. She got back into her car quickly and sped away, but her fingers wouldn't work. She couldn't hold the steering wheel, and drove on only by placing palm pressure against the wheel. Her fingers cramped, and that scared her as she wondered if she was hurt and in shock.

Two miles south of the church, her motor seized up and heavy smoke filled under the hood. She couldn't move, and saw many police, fire and ambulances racing past her on the other side of the road towards the church. She knew something awful had happened. Someone named Jenny stopped to check on her. Christina told her what had happened, and Jenny said she would call for help. Minutes later firemen showed up and helped her. Then an officer stayed with her for several hours. She had not been hit, but her car was totaled due to the engine and body damage caused by the bullets.[47]

As the shooter crossed the road behind Christina's vehicle, he turned his attention again to his right towards another approaching vehicle.

Matt Purcell was driving along the east side of the church as well. Just as Clayton Meininger had done a few seconds before, Matt turned south at the northeast corner of the building and was southbound between the main building and the Tent right behind Christina Wilke. Matt's wife Judy was in the passenger seat beside him. Chelsea York, a 23-year-old missionary staying with them at the time was behind Judy. The Purcell's 16-year-old daughter Kayla was behind Matt, and 12-year-old daughter Kristen was between Kayla and Chelsea.

They heard pops then saw a young girl and guy rush into the tent. Matt stopped the car to evaluate what was going on, as they saw a young man in all black gear carrying a rifle by the east doors of the main building. Kristen thought at first it was a friend with a paintball gun. They watched as something fell out of his rifle (detectives later retrieved a spent 30 round magazine from the area just outside the east doors)[48], then they all saw him bring the rifle up and take aim at them.

As he raised the rifle, he shot through the front windshield from six to eight feet away. As Matt yelled for everyone to get down he tried to race away, but the car stalled. The gunman calmly walked up to the right side and the passenger side window exploded as he fired again. In the adrenalin-charged chaos of those tense moments, some in the family thought Matt got out of the car until they yelled for him to get back in. Whether he ever got out or not (he probably did based on Roy Pollete's statements), he got the car started, and slammed it into gear so hard he broke the gearshift off the steering column.

As they raced away the girls could see blood on their mother and glass in her face. They discovered she had been shot through the right shoulder. Matt rushed her to Penrose Hospital where she was treated and released that evening.[49]

Detectives found many bullet holes in their Toyota Sequoia. The front passenger window had been shot through, was shattered and most of the glass had fallen out of it. The rear driver's side window was shattered as well. A bullet gash in the hood indicated an angled bullet path of front passenger to rear driver side. A bullet hole through the front windshield indicated the same projection. The passenger side mirror was hit, as well as the door. Each of those indicated a more straight across bullet path of passenger to driver, but still with a slight angle backwards. The inside of the driver's side door had a bullet hole, and a bullet had gone through the driver's side headrest from front to back. The driver's side seat showed evidence that a bullet had skimmed across between it and the driver.[50]

But the Purcell family and their guest had been spared.

• • •

Buck Snodgrass and Dave Hagen had been investigating the smoke at the north entry. As they walked back towards the desk inside, Buck commented to Dave that he didn't like this. Things didn't feel right at all to the experienced Vietnam combat veteran. Then they heard faint shots outside to the east. Both knew what it was, and Dave spoke it first -- almost as a question -- "that's gunshots?" Both men took off quickly up the long hallway towards the shooting.

The outside shots were muffled enough that many others thought they were hearing different things. Some thought it was stacks of tables or chairs being knocked over, ice falling from the roof, trash cans being knocked over or firecrackers. As with many crowded environment shootings, many thought it was a skit.

Buck and Dave were certain enough when they heard the sound, to quickly move towards it even though neither had yet been authorized to carry weapons on security duty. When they were a fair way up the hallway towards the outside sounds, they saw the shooter step into view through the exterior doors and it was immediately obvious he was shooting an assault rifle. They watched him turn the weapon towards them, and saw the glass in the door in front of them explode. He had turned to come in and was firing through the glass doors into the hallway as he did so.

Both men spun around and started a commanding sweep to get everyone out of the hallway. They yelled as loudly as they could as the shooter was by then shooting through breaking glass down the long hallway. With hard quarry tile floors, and sheetrock walls and ceilings, the hallway became a booming echo chamber as bullets zinged past Buck and Dave as they ran yelling for people to get out. These were probably the shots and yells I first heard at the far end and upper level of the building where I was behind doors in the executive wing.

Those with little or no expectation of malice are caught by total surprise when it happens. Just as Christina Wilke had trouble associating sights and sounds with danger, so did many unsuspecting people inside the building. A mother told me later, that as the shots were booming through the hallway Buck and Dave were clearing, her son argued back to them that he didn't want to quit the computer game he was about to win. But with no time to spare, when they heard his resistance she told me her son heard authority like never before and quickly obeyed. Neither Buck nor Dave could recall the young man, but he will never forget them.

But something happened as the shooter came through the outer doors and stood in the breezeway just before coming through the inside set of doors, that is nearly beyond comprehension.

55-year-old Diane Cole was working as a janitor cleaning a restroom right beside those doors. Her helper and son-in-law Craig Langer was just a little way down the hallway when the interior shooting and hallway clearing started. Craig couldn't believe what he saw happen next.[51]

Diane heard sounds like cracking and popping, so she came out of the restroom. She saw broken glass all over the floor, and saw a young man standing on the other side of the door the glass had obviously came out of. Diane walked over to the door and asked the young man, "Did you see that!?" She was obviously upset that someone had broken the door, and was probably a bit suspect of and angry towards the young man standing there who was not answering her.

When she looked up at him expecting some kind of response, she saw him cocking his head to one side like a confused dog trying to understand. Then she saw him raise his rifle and point it straight at her. Then it all came together, and she ran screaming down the hallway as he yelled vulgarities and fired down the hallway in her direction.[52]

As Buck and Dave made it to the far end of the hallway, Dave took a right turn and exited the building down hallway one running out towards his vehicle to retrieve his Glock. Buck made it to the far end of the hallway then turned around to face the shooter. Squatted low with his arms spread wide to his sides, he was signaling and yelling at people to stay back as he kept eyes on the shooter. As soon as he directed me towards the shooter, Buck ran out the north main entry towards his truck to retrieve his Ruger P235 .45 ACP.

Jeanne Assam had seen the first smoke bomb, called the fire department and taken statements from some who had reported seeing it tossed. As she had been taking the information, someone told her of a second smoke bomb on the south side of the building. When she heard questionable pops outside the building, she too went east towards the sound. There was a lot to process as she tried to make sense of the smoke and sounds, and determine the source and / or sources of threats. It felt as though there were threats converging from all sides. As the gunfire came into the building, prompting Buck and Dave to clear the hallway, Jeanne took cover and prepared in hallway 160 on the south side of the main hall. One of the double hallway doors was open and the other closed, so she took cover behind the one that was closed.

After the gunman shot at Larry, Jeanne heard the shooting stop and it sounded as if he was reloading. She stepped around the closed door yelling at the gunman to drop his weapon. This probably took him by surprise as his attention would have been on Larry down the hall. When he refused to drop his weapon, and instead began moving in hostile manners, Jeanne fired 10 rapid fire shots from 29 yards away with her 9 mm, and watched as the shooter dropped to the floor.[53]

The assault was over

The entire attack was exceptionally brief. Officers Wyatt, Chacon and Roman had just left the campus. Joe Wyatt had switched his radio off[54], Roman and Chacon had their radios still on. When the call came over the radio, Chacon was just 1.1 miles south of the church. The church was still within easy view where he turned around and began racing back towards the church. As he accelerated to code 3 with lights flashing he asked for Roman's position. His question was answered when Roman roared past him. On a normal day at posted speed limits it takes 1.5 minutes from that intersection to the east doors of the church.

The scene had changed a lot from when they had left moments earlier. Crowds of people were running to their cars, cars were speeding out of the parking lot, and people were running towards other buildings, but everyone was leaving the main building. Their attention was drawn immediately to the east side, as they quickly retrieved tactical gear from their vehicles and started towards those doors. As they approached they saw an EPSO officer approaching as well. Chacon radioed he was forming a 3 man joint-agency team and that they were going in[55]. CSPD Officer Price was pulling in right behind them. He jumped out of his car, threw on his tactical gear, and ran towards them. He brought up the rear as the 4 man team entered the church[56]. They saw me standing with my arms out directing them to the downed shooter.

Some years before, the church had bought some cheap CCTV cameras. The images were not clear enough for any kind of criminal conviction or even facial recognition of familiar people, but time stamps at least revealed when something happened. At 13:10 that afternoon a woman is seen casually pushing her baby in a stroller inside the Tent building. At 13:10:24 the woman suddenly jolted (obviously alarmed by something) quickly pulled her baby carriage back towards herself, turned and exited to the left of the frame.

It is reasonable to assume that was the first sounds of gunfire in the parking lot.

At 13:10:51 a camera on the inside of the main building revealed similar surprise as several people in that main reception area are seen instantly taking a crouching position. It would have been 27 seconds after those in the Tent had heard shooting, that it became apparent in the center of the main building. At 13:11:07 an individual is seen clearing the area from the west end of the hallway. This would likely be Buck, and would indicate it took him and Dave 16 seconds to clear the hallway once the shooter began shooting into the building. It would have also been about 16 seconds from the time I heard the shots in the building before coming into Buck's view.

By 13:11:26 all motion had stopped, and there was no further recording until an individual ran in from outside and up the hallway at 13:14:24[57]. It is likely that was Buck, but may have been Mike Steczo. It was over when each of those men came in. So at the very most, the shooting lasted four minutes exactly, but most likely closer to, or less than three total minutes. By 13:17:55 Jeanne enters into the frame with her gun still drawn. It was some minutes after the shooting when Dave pointed out that her weapon was still drawn, saying, "It will be a lot safer if you have that gun holstered when the police get here."[58]

A little known development overlooked by many was how fast a force of defenders was coming together. Neither Jeanne nor I knew the other was there when we chose our respective defensive positions. But had

141

the shooter defeated Jeanne he would have faced me. Had he defeated me, he would have faced Buck coming back in with his .45. Had Buck been defeated, Dave would have been coming in about then with his weapon. About the same time Dave re-entered the building, Mike was coming in from the WPC. So in a very short amount of time there were five layers of armed defenders getting into positions to stop the killer.

• • •

SUICIDE?

When Jeanne and I were looking down at the shooter, it appeared as though the blood was spraying from the right side of his neck. The coroner's report however only listed one bullet wound above his shoulders, and that was through the upper back of his head from his mouth. The coroner determined the fatal shot was self-inflicted, due in part to powder burns around his mouth indicating close proximity when fired. I recall only one rapid fire volley of rounds with no follow up. But when it was over, there were ten 9 mm casings with a head stamp of "Luger PC" (matching Jeanne's ammunition) and one empty 9 mm casing with a head stamp of "Luger RP" (matching the casings still in the clip from the weapon cleared by Larry). [59]

The shooter had bullet wounds on his left leg, left wrist and hand, chest and the one through his head. Both weapons had been struck, and some bullet holes were in the wall around him and in a set of folding glass doors to the shooter's right (indicating bullet travel from Jeanne's position). I believe the coroner's report proves that the fatal shot was from his own firearm, but we will never know if it was intentional or accidental as Jeanne was hitting him hard and fast.

What we do know is that Jeanne Assam stopped the killer 60 feet inside the building. Jeanne is a petite woman, but when I saw her appear out of nowhere across the hallway that day with her weapon drawn, she looked 12 feet tall and was obviously in command. Both her law enforcement training and personal intensity were obvious as she surprised the shooter from an angle he was not prepared for. With the authority enveloping her in those critical moments, she crushed the momentum of evil.

Our team was ready. Not as ready as we wish we had been. Every one of us wish we could have been right there when he pulled that weapon out of his trunk. Every one of us would have done some things differently had we known what was about to happen. Many young people died that day (considering the Arvada attack as well) and good families were changed forever. Every one of us would have done anything for that to not be part of the story.

In the end, "The horse is made ready for the day of battle, but victory rests with the Lord."[60] The day did not go as any of us would have wanted. But it did not go as the shooter had intended either. We have no misconceptions regarding Who was ultimately in charge that day. The shooter had the capacity, opportunity and intention of fulfilling his threat that, "Christian America – this is your Columbine."

In that regard he failed, due at least in part, to an intentional security plan.

References

1 Department of Justice, Bureau of Justice Statistics, Homicide Trends in the U.S., Multiple Victims and Offenders

2 The 9/11 Commission Report, Final Report of the National Commission on Terrorist Attacks Upon the United States. Official Government Edition.

3 Nehemiah 4:9 (NIV)

4 Nehemiah 4: 17 (NIV)

5 "Hello Charlie – Letters From a Serial Killer" by: Charlie Hess and Davin Seay. Atria Books

6 CDC Lightning-Associated Deaths -- United States, 1980-1995 MMWR 47(19);391-394

7 U.S. Structure Fires in Educational Properties, Jennifer D. Flynn, NFPA, Quincy, MA August 2007

8 National School Safety Center's Report on School Associated Violent Deaths

9 National School Safety Center's Report on School Associated Violent Deaths

10 Fire Loss in The United States for 2010, By NFPA (Michael J. Karter, Jr. September 2011)

11 U.S. Religious and Funeral Property Structure Fires, Marty Ahrens, NFPA Fire Analysis and Research, Quincy, MA, June 2010.

12 NCATF "The National Church Arson Task Force Church Threat Assessment Guide"

13 "Pastors at Risk" by: H. B. London and Neil Wiseman, page 22

14 U.S. Conference of Catholic Bishops, Charter for the Protection of Children and Young People. Copyright © 2002

15 II Timothy 4:14-18 (NIV)

16 Denver Westword News, October 9, 1997 "Out of Focus"

17 Proverbs 16:18, (NASB)

18 Alan Cooperman, LA Times & Washington Post, 11/5/2006

19 Matthew 6:25 (NIV)

20 U.S. Department of Labor, Evacuation Plans and Procedures E-Tool

21 Message by Dr. Stephen Trammell as he was quoting a friend at the Texas Ministry Conference on 2/15/2012

22 CSPD CASE REPORT 07-40399 NARRATIVE SUPPLEMENT BY B. Pratt / 2422, Lt. Mark Smith / 75 and CC interview with FBI agent D. Shannon

23 Arvada Police Report

24 Arvada Police Report and CSPD CASE REPORT 07-40399 NARRATIVE SUPPLEMENT BY B. Pratt / 2422

25 CSPD CASE REPORT 07-40399 NARRATIVE SUPPLEMENT BY P. W. Quick / 1502

26 CSPD CASE REPORT 07-40399 NARRATIVE SUPPLEMENT BY L. Herbert / 388

27 CSPD CASE REPORT 07-40399 NARRATIVE SUPPLEMENT BY L. Herbert / 388

28 CSPD CASE REPORT 07-40399 NARRATIVE SUPPLEMENT BY D Thompson / 2062

29 CSPD CASE REPORT 07-40399 NARRATIVE SUPPLEMENT BY R. Gyson / 42

30 "Gone in a Heartbeat – Our Daughters Died...Our Faith Endures", By David & Marie Works. Page 79

31 CSPD CASE REPORT 07-40399 NARRATIVE SUPPLEMENT BY J. Armas / 2740

32 CSPD CASE REPORT 07-40399 NARRATIVE SUPPLEMENT BY Ransom / 2896 and D. Pratt / 974

33 CSPD CASE REPORT 07-40399 NARRATIVE SUPPLEMENT BY L. Herbert / 388,

34 CSPD CASE REPORT 07-40399 NARRATIVE SUPPLEMENT BY F. B. Walker / 9612 and D. Krueger / 1962

35 CSPD CASE REPORT 07-40399 NARRATIVE SUPPLEMENT BY C. Rivera / 1766

36 CSPD CASE REPORT 07-40399 NARRATIVE SUPPLEMENT BY R. Gysin / 1247, A. Romine / 1967and M. Chacon / 2300

37 CSPD CASE REPORT 07-40399 NARRATIVE SUPPLEMENT BY P. Gurnett / 2656 and E, Ingalsbe / 2051

38 CSPD CASE REPORT 07-40399 NARRATIVE SUPPLEMENT BY B. K. Strickland / 1509

39 Colorado Springs 911 tapes released to public

40 CSPD CASE REPORT 07-40399 NARRATIVE SUPPLEMENT BY W. E. Burrell / 56

41 Blog forum posting on ex-pentecostal.com by nghtmrchld26 posted 12/07/07 (since removed)

42 Blog forum posting on Independent Spirits (since removed) by Chrstnghtmr on 9/04/06 according to Eric Gorski, Associated Press 12/13/07 in article titled *Colorado Church Gunman Left Twisted Trail* AUTHOR'S NOTE: A spokesperson for shooter's family denied the incident he wrote of ever happened. However in her interview with Arvada Detectie VanderVeen -- Arvada Police Report page 294 -- the shooter's mother recounted the story

43 Blog forum posting on Independent Spirits (since removed) by Chrstnghtmr on 12/12/07 according to Eric Gorski, Associated Press 12/13/07 in article titled *Colorado Church Gunman Left Twisted Trail*

44 CSPD CASE REPORT 07-40399 NARRATIVE SUPPLEMENT BY Jennene J. Scott / 1506

45 "Gone in a Heartbeat – Our Daughters Died…Our Faith Endures", By David & Marie Works. Pages 57-59

46 CSPD CASE REPORT 07-40399 NARRATIVE SUPPLEMENT BY K. Mareshah Hale / 1755, Corey Thompson / 1872, G. Pring / 510 and P. W. Quick / 1502

47 CSPD CASE REPORT 07-40399 NARRATIVE SUPPLEMENT BY J. A. Garrett / 12 and K. E. Gustavson / 2151

48 CSPD CASE REPORT 07-40399 NARRATIVE SUPPLEMENT BY A. Roman / 1343

49 CSPD CASE REPORT 07-40399 NARRATIVE SUPPLEMENT BY W. Listul / 429, Gina Seago / 1507 and E, K. Anderson / 1386 and P. W. Quick / 1502

50 CSPD CASE REPORT 07-40399 NARRATIVE SUPPLEMENT BY C. O`Conner / 2057, W. Listul / 429, B. Dehart / 82 and P. W. Quick / 1502

51 CSPD CASE REPORT 07-40399 NARRATIVE SUPPLEMENT BY P. Gurnett / 2656

52 CSPD CASE REPORT 07-40399 NARRATIVE SUPPLEMENT BY M. Black / 1775

53 CSPD CASE REPORT 07-40399 NARRATIVE SUPPLEMENT BY M. Happ / 1102

54 CSPD CASE REPORT 07-40399 NARRATIVE SUPPLEMENT BY J. Wyatt / 32

55 CSPD CASE REPORT 07-40399 NARRATIVE SUPPLEMENT BY A. Roman / 1343, M. Chacon / 2300 and J. Wyatt / 32

56 CSPD CASE REPORT 07-40399 NARRATIVE SUPPLEMENT BY E. Price / 2316

57 CSPD CASE REPORT 07-40399 NARRATIVE SUPPLEMENT BY R. D. Curtis / 1696

58 Dave Hagen e-mail to his son and cc to Carl Chinn, capturing his recollections written shortly days after the incident.

59 CSPD CASE REPORT 07-40399 NARRATIVE SUPPLEMENT BY R. Gyson / 42 and M. Happ / 1102

60 Proverbs 21:31, (NIV)

About the Author

Carl Chinn dismissed the importance of physical security through much of his early career, considering it an inconvenient distraction of debatable value. Then he faced an angry gunman in a ministry, which changed his views. It would turn out to be the first of two gunmen he encountered at ministries.

Following the first attacker's trial in 1996, Chinn began researching and writing on the subject of North American ministry incidents – especially criminal acts. He maintains a website (www.carlchinn.com) on the subject and speaks at related conferences. He has been featured in national media and publications including Focus on the Family, The 700 Club, Preaching Magazine, Christianity Today, Moody Bible Institute and radio interviews. He has spoken at colleges, seminaries, churches, ASIS, and various charitable events. He is a frequent speaker for the National Organization of Church Security & Safety Management. In 2009, the Washington Post credited his website as the most comprehensive collection of deadly force incidents at ministries available.

The author and his wife raised five children in the Colorado Springs area, and currently enjoy nine grandchildren.